# Co-Parenting With a Narcissistic Ex

Setting Boundaries, Eliminating Conflict,
Healing From Narcissistic Abuse,
Protecting Your Children, and
Finding Peace

D1738126

**Olivia Clarke**

Get the latest on new releases, free content and special promotions sent straight to your inbox! Sign up for our monthly news letter to stay updated with Rocket Publishing Group and Olivia Clarke.

# Table of Contents

# Introduction

I want to start by saying I'm proud of you. Choosing to leave a relationship with a narcissist or someone with narcissistic traits takes a lot of guts and strength, especially if you've had children together. It's a big deal, and you should give yourself major credit for taking this step to create a better life for yourself and your children.

I know from my own experience and work as a mental health professional that the pain of leaving a toxic relationship is intense and complicated. If you haven't been through it yourself or don't have the right knowledge, it can be difficult to understand what someone in this situation is going through. When children are involved in a situation like this, it becomes even more confusing. One minute you might feel relieved and empowered, and the next you're wondering if you did the right thing. Trust me, it's normal to feel this way.

It's okay if not everyone understands what you're going through. What matters is that you're making progress, even if it feels small. Every step you take towards creating a healthier, happier life for you and your kids is something to celebrate. Don't ever forget that choosing to leave is always better than staying stuck in a bad situation.

When you have children with a narcissist, you can't just cut ties completely. You're going to have to find a way to co-parent with your ex while also trying to heal from all the hurt they caused you. It's a lot to handle, but that's where this book comes in. I want to share some practical tools and strategies that can help you keep your focus on your kids and their well-being, even when things get tough.

I've been where you are, and I've made plenty of mistakes along the way. But I've also learned a lot, and I want to share that with you. Think of this book as a roadmap, with insights from both my work as a therapist and my personal journey.

Together, we'll tackle the challenges of co-parenting with a narcissistic ex head-on. We'll talk about how to communicate better, set healthy boundaries, and ensure your kids' emotional needs are being met. We'll also dive into the importance of taking care of yourself and healing from the trauma of narcissistic abuse because you can't be the best parent possible if you're running on empty.

Most importantly, I want you to know that you're not alone. By picking up this book, you've already shown that you're ready to take control of your life and break free from the cycle of abuse. That's a major step, and I'm honored to be part of your support system. I promise to give you the guidance, understanding, and practical tools you need to thrive.

So let's do this together, one step at a time. You've got this, and I've got your back.

# Chapter 1:

# Understanding the Narcissist

Sophie was hooked by Niel's charm from the start. She found his confidence magnetic, even if he did love to constantly talk about his accomplishments and talents. Sophie hardly got a word in when they went on a date, but she enjoyed listening to him speak.

During the first few months, Niel showered her with attention and compliments, making her feel like the most special woman in the world.

But before long, the cracks started showing. Niel became petulant and cold anytime Sophie paid attention to her friends or work, telling her that he should be her priority. He accused her of being selfish despite Sophie constantly rearranging her schedule for his needs. "This is how you treat me after all I've done for you?" he'd complain.

Niel was also obsessed with his own importance and achievements. It made him furious if Sophie gave him any kind of advice. "I don't tell you how to live your small, sad life," he'd snap. If she pushed back, he only became more venomous, calling her ungrateful and inferior.

Over time, Niel's callousness and air of superiority chipped away at Sophie's self-esteem. She found herself anxiously modeling her behavior to his moods, scared to trigger another temper outburst. When she attended events with him, she felt he was exhibiting a trophy on his arm, rather than bringing a supportive partner.

When Sophie had to deal with a family tragedy, Niel went silent and was completely inattentive to her emotional turmoil. "I have my own issues," he coldly remarked when she reached out for comfort. It was clear her pain was not on his list of priorities.

Sophie realized this was simply how Niel viewed the world—his priority was to satisfy his own insatiable narcissistic needs. Her emotions, ambitions, and identity only mattered to him in how they inflated his ego. She decided to end the relationship, and her only regret was that she hadn't walked away from his twisted sense of superiority sooner.

# What Is a Narcissist?

If your ex is a narcissist, you probably wish you had known more about it before getting involved with them. However, once you understand what narcissism is really about, it is easier to deal with them. You will recognize the self-centered pattern of behavior as we consider all the characteristics of a narcissist.

They think they should be the center of your and anyone else's universe, as they believe in their own importance. They'll take advantage of you without feeling guilty about it. While they want your attention and sympathy, you'll quickly become aware of their lack of empathy when things go wrong. Don't expect them to be your shoulder to cry on, though they'll quickly confront you if they feel you're not there to support them during tough times.

All of us have some narcissistic traits, and we can all be self-absorbed or arrogant at times. These traits are usually mild and don't dominate your personality. However, those with full-blown narcissistic personality disorder (NPD) exhibit these narcissistic patterns in an extreme way, which affects their day-to-day lives.

Although there is obviously no excuse for mistreating others, narcissism could be the result of childhood trauma. Narcissism can develop as a coping mechanism to deal with a dysfunctional family life.

A lack of genuine affection, emotional abuse, conditional love based on high expectations, exploitation, or growing up with narcissistic parents can all contribute to developing a narcissistic personality. Traumatic childhood environments can instill deep insecurities that narcissistic behaviors like arrogance, entitlement, and demanding excessive admiration and attention help to compensate for. Narcissists are usually insecure people who are afraid of being rejected and abandoned.

By constantly putting down others, narcissists can manage their feelings of inadequacy and gain a sense of being in control.

## The Different Types of Narcissists

While categorizations can help you understand narcissism, it's important to remember people can exhibit traits from all the different categories.

### The Grandiose Narcissist

The grandiose narcissist has all the classic traits—an overinflated ego, a constant need for admiration, and a lack of empathy. They tend to dominate conversations, and they like to brag and name-drop.

When it comes to parenting, they tend to view their children as trophies or extensions of themselves, not as individuals in their own right. They are the ultimate critics, and discipline is all about upholding their rigid expectations and rules. The kids shouldn't dare to disappoint or embarrass them.

When the child's achievements make the grandiose narcissist look good, they will idolize their child. However, as soon as the child disappoints them, for example, by not achieving academically or on the sports field, the lack of empathy and devaluation will kick in. The child is simply there to help them meet their needs for admiration and ego gratification, and they're not concerned about the child's emotional well-being.

During a divorce, this type of narcissist can use their children as weapons for power and attention. They don't care about the impact on the children and only want to be seen as the superior, most committed parent, while you become the villain. They can bad-mouth you to the children, or start giving them excessive gifts to show them what amazing parents they are.

### The Vulnerable Narcissist

The vulnerable narcissists are the insecure ones who are always fishing for compliments and reassurance.

As a parent, the vulnerable narcissist needs constant validation that they're doing a great job. This could be the mom who posts a million pics on social media of her kids' activities, eagerly awaiting all the praise. Or the dad who overcompensates by chauffeuring the kids everywhere, desperately wanting them to acknowledge his efforts.

They are usually inconsistent when it comes to applying discipline. One moment they're a strict disciplinarian to prove their authority. The next, they're pushovers, so the kids will keep loving them. The truth is that they crave adoration from their children.

Children quickly learn that calming their parent's moods means complimenting and reassuring them. These parents can be endlessly needy for ego-stroking.

After a divorce, things can get even rockier. The vulnerable narcissist may keep traumatizing the kids by constantly seeking their allegiance and approval. They often sabotage the other parent's time with the kids and play the victim by complaining that their children were taken from them.

It's really confusing for the kids—one moment this needy parent wants to be their best friend; the next they're making resentful comments about having to sacrifice for ungrateful children. The children are always walking on eggshells, trying fruitlessly to stabilize these fragile egos that are never satisfied.

## The Covert Narcissist

The covert narcissist tends to fly under the radar, making them difficult to identify. At first, they seem humble and unassuming—maybe even a little insecure or self-deprecating. However, deep down, they're just as grandiose as the loud, obnoxious narcissists. They've just got a different way of getting their ego stroked.

As a parent, the covert narcissist is the master of the backhanded compliment. "Wow, you actually managed to do that homework all by yourself? I'm so proud!" They can tear you down while pretending to build you up.

These parents are also really good at playing the martyr—making you feel endlessly guilty about all they sacrifice, even as they criticize your efforts.

After a divorce, the covert narcissist could seem like a reasonable parent at first. This is just their way of being passive-aggressive and maintaining control. Were you unable to attend the last parent-teacher conference? Prepare for their complaints about how they have to do everything alone.

They tend to use subtle emotional manipulation when it comes to the children. While they will ignore bad behavior one day, they'll blow up over something tiny to ensure the child feels off-balance and insecure. It's about conditioning the children to need their approval.

This type of narcissist feels morally and intellectually superior so they belittle their children and leave them second-guessing themselves and wanting their approval. It's covert control cloaked in false modesty—a toxic combination.

## The Communal Narcissist

The communal narcissist can be a tricky one to spot, especially when it comes to parenting. On the surface, they seem like the most selfless, devoted mom or dad around. They could be that parent who's always volunteering for every school activity and charity drive. Or the one who repeatedly talks about all the sacrifices they make for their kids.

However, when you look closer, you'll realize it's just an ego game. The communal narcissistic parent enjoys the praise and admiration for being so generous and involved. It makes them feel important and superior to other parents.

It can seem they're keeping score of every good deed and every chore and childcare task they take on. And they'll rub the other parent's nose in it. The underlying message is "Look what an amazing parent I am!" If the children don't show enough appreciation and gratitude for their sacrifices, they'll pull out the martyr act and guilt trips.

After a divorce, the communal narcissist may try to win the admiration of teachers, coaches, and other parents. It becomes important to be seen as a devoted single parent. They could also start love-bombing the kids with extra activities and gifts.

The children may start feeling like objects to be accumulated and shown off. The constant sense of being used to feed the narcissistic parent's ego can take an emotional toll on the children.

## The Malignant Narcissist

The malignant narcissist is the worst of the bunch—a toxic blend of arrogance, aggression, and a complete lack of empathy. When it comes to parenting, they can turn the lives of their partner and children into a living hell.

This type wants to dominate, control, and extract constant supply from their kids. Malignant narcissists will shamelessly manipulate their children's emotions to get what they want. Their love is conditional and is usually only given in exchange for adoration and obedience.

They rule the roost through fear and favor. One moment you're the golden child receiving positive attention from them, the next you're the scapegoat being raged at and demeaned over the smallest perceived slight. If you live with a malignant narcissist, you're constantly walking on eggshells.

Physical and emotional abuse is common, but they're masters at victim-blaming, so the children end up feeling crazy and at fault. "Look what you made me do!" Any attempt at rebellion or healthy boundaries is met with severe punishment.

After a divorce, the malignant narcissist will weaponize the children against the other parent through nasty smear campaigns, brainwashing the kids against the other parent, and even putting the children in physical danger during their custody time—it's all fair game if it feeds their sick need for vengeance.

They'll flip between love-bombing the kids with expensive gifts and verbally abusive meltdowns during which they can call the children terrible names. This creates complex trauma bonds where the kids crave any form of attention or approval from them.

In many ways, malignant narcissists treat their children more like possessions than people. They see them as tools to exploit or weapons against people who defy them.

All narcissists are damaging in their own way. But this type takes it to extremes with their combination of entitlement, lack of empathy, and willingness to be cruel against their children. If you're dealing with this type of narcissist, your children need to be protected against this toxic dynamic.

# The Difference Between Narcissistic Personality Disorder (NPD) and Narcissistic Traits

Narcissistic traits and narcissistic personality disorder (NPD) exist on a spectrum. Everyone has some narcissistic qualities to a certain degree, but when those traits become excessive and problematic, it may indicate a more serious condition like NPD.

## *When Is NPD Diagnosed?*

The key factors that differentiate narcissistic traits from NPD are the severity, pervasiveness, and functional impairment caused by narcissistic behaviors.

A person could be diagnosed with NPD if their narcissistic traits meet the following criteria:

- The narcissistic patterns of thinking and behavior are pervasive, meaning they are present across various situations and contexts, not just occasional or isolated incidents. These traits are deeply ingrained in the person's personality and worldview.

- The narcissistic traits in NPD are severe and extreme, going far beyond ordinary levels of confidence or self-importance. Individuals with NPD exhibit a grandiose sense of self-importance, a profound lack of empathy, and an excessive need for admiration and entitlement.

- NPD causes significant challenges in important areas of life, such as personal relationships, work, or academic performance. The narcissist tends to lose jobs and relationships. These behaviors interfere with the person's ability to function effectively in social, occupational, or other important settings.

- Unlike normal narcissistic traits that can be flexible and situational, the narcissistic patterns in NPD are rigid and inflexible. The person can't change their behavior or worldview, even when there is evidence that challenges their perception.

- The narcissistic traits in NPD cause significant distress or impairment in the person's life or the lives of those around them. This might include strained relationships, difficulty keeping a job, or emotional distress.

The diagnosis of NPD is typically made by a mental health professional, such as a psychologist or psychiatrist, through a comprehensive evaluation that considers the patterns of behavior, thoughts, and emotional experiences over an extended period.

## *What Are Narcissistic Traits?*

Sarah is a proud mother who loves bragging about her son's accomplishments to her friends and family. She often posts pictures and updates about his achievements on social media, hoping for admiration and praise. While Sarah can be a bit boastful at times, she is usually able to provide her son with the love, support, and encouragement he needs. Her narcissistic tendencies do not significantly impact her ability to be a good parent.

Tom is a father with NPD. He has an extreme sense of entitlement and believes that his children's sole purpose is to make him look good and bring him admiration. Tom constantly compares his children to others, belittling them if they don't meet his unrealistic expectations. He favors his older child, who excels academically, and often neglects or berates his younger child for not living up to his standards.

Tom struggles to empathize with his children's feelings or acknowledge their individual needs. He frequently interrupts them, talks over them, and makes decisions for them without asking them what they really want. His behavior has led to emotional distress and low self-esteem in his children and has strained his relationships with them and his partner.

Tom's narcissistic parenting style has the potential to cause long-lasting emotional and psychological harm to his children.

A parent with NPD will struggle to provide the unconditional love, support, and empathy their children need. They could also emotionally abuse or exploit their children, either using them as sources of admiration or narcissistic supply.

# Narcissists That Make the Worst Parents

When it comes to the types of narcissists that tend to be the worst parents, malignant narcissists are probably the most damaging and toxic.

## *The Sadistic Malignant Narcissistic Parent*

Malignant narcissists exhibit a dangerous combination of traits that can make them particularly harmful as parents.

Like other narcissists, this type of parent puts themselves on a pedestal, believing they are superior to everyone else, including their child. This parent may demand constant praise, admiration, and obedience from their child, and they become angry, punishing the child if they don't get what they want.

Not only that, but this type of parent also lacks empathy and compassion for their child's feelings and needs. They may be emotionally or even physically abusive, belittling or humiliating their child. Their primary concern is feeding their ego and maintaining control, regardless of the emotional toll it takes on the child.

Unlike other types of narcissists who may simply be self-absorbed or insecure, malignant narcissists can exhibit sadistic tendencies, taking pleasure in exploiting and manipulating their child for their own gain. If they have more than one child, they can pit them against each other, play mind games, and intentionally undermine their children's self-worth.

Children raised by these types of parents often grow up feeling worthless, anxious, and emotionally scarred. They may struggle with low self-esteem and trust issues and have difficulty forming healthy relationships later in life.

While all forms of narcissistic parenting can be damaging, the combination of grandiose self-importance, lack of empathy, and their potential for sadistic behavior make malignant narcissists particularly toxic and detrimental to a child's emotional and psychological well-being.

## *The Manipulative Covert Narcissistic Parent*

Covert narcissists are more subtle and passive-aggressive in their narcissistic behaviors.

One of the main issues with covert narcissistic parents is that they often parent-ify their children. This means they rely on their kids to meet their own emotional needs and seek excessive validation from them. The child can become like an emotional "husband" or "wife".

For example, a covert narcissistic parent may constantly complain about their problems or marital issues to the child, burdening them with inappropriate levels of emotional responsibility. They may also fish for compliments or reassurance from the child, making the child feel like they have to take care of the parent's fragile ego.

Covert narcissists are also skilled at manipulation, often using guilt-tripping, gaslighting, or playing the victim to control their children's behavior and ensure their own needs are met. They may invalidate their child's feelings or experiences, or make the child feel responsible for their own emotional well-being.

Children of covert narcissistic parents often grow up feeling emotionally neglected, despite the parent's apparent vulnerability or neediness. They may struggle with a lack of boundaries, as their own identities and needs are consistently disregarded or overshadowed by the parent's demands.

While overt grandiose narcissists may be more overtly domineering or abusive, covert narcissists can be just as damaging, if not more so, due to the insidious nature of their manipulation and the emotional enmeshment they create with their children.

# Activity: Analyzing Your Narcissistic Ex's Behavior

The objective of this activity is to help you better understand your narcissistic ex-partner's behavior and its impact on your past relationship.

## Instructions

Think about your past relationship with your narcissistic ex and identify three to five instances where their behavior caused you distress or confusion.

Write down a detailed description of what happened in every situation, including

- the context of the situation
- your ex's specific actions or words
- your emotional response and thoughts at the time
- the impact of their behavior on you and the relationship

After writing down each occurrence, analyze the patterns of narcissistic behavior by answering the following questions:

**Which narcissistic traits did your ex display in this situation (e.g. lack of empathy, grandiosity, manipulation, gaslighting)?**

**How did their behavior make you feel, and why?**

Did you notice recurring themes or tactics your ex used across different situations?

How did their behavior affect your self-esteem, mental health, and overall well-being?

Did you address your ex's behavior and their response to your concerns?

Did you express your feelings and needs clearly?

Did your ex acknowledge your concerns or dismiss them?

Did they make genuine efforts to change their behavior or offer insincere apologies?

Identify any red flags or warning signs you might have overlooked during the relationship that could help you recognize narcissistic behavior in the future.

Based on your analysis, write a letter to your past self in which you offer yourself guidance and support. Acknowledge the challenges you faced and the strength it took to leave the relationship.

End the activity by writing about the lessons you've learned and the personal growth you've experienced since the relationship ended. How can this knowledge help you create healthier relationships in the future?

# Key Takeaways

- Narcissists exhibit a pattern of self-centered, arrogant behavior with a lack of empathy for others.

- Narcissistic traits may develop as a coping mechanism from childhood trauma, emotional abuse, or narcissistic parenting.

- Although there are different types of narcissists, they share similar characteristics.

- As parents, narcissists may view children as extensions of themselves, criticize them harshly, or use them for attention/ego gratification.

- After divorce, narcissistic parents may bad-mouth the other parent to kids, be inconsistent with discipline, or try to turn kids against the other parent.

- Children of narcissistic parents often feel used, criticized, and emotionally manipulated, needing to walk on eggshells to avoid angering the narcissistic parent.

In Chapter 2, we'll look at how you can process your emotions in difficult situations.

# Chapter 2:

# Processing Emotions

The feelings came in waves after Cynthia finally worked up the courage to leave her narcissistic ex-husband. One moment, she felt an overwhelming sense of relief and confidence that she had made the right decision to get herself and her children out of that toxic situation. However, the doubts and regrets came crashing in like a tidal wave. What if she had tried harder? Was she too rash? Maybe if she had been more patient and understanding, he would have changed. The intense feelings of confusion left her feeling completely unmoored.

She had become so isolated from her friends and family over the years because his controlling behavior pushed them all away. Now that she was finally free, she found herself feeling anxious. She kept questioning her choice. How would she support herself and the kids? What mind games would he try to play during the custody battle? Some days the heaviness was so strong that she couldn't get out of bed, enveloped in numbness.

Other times anger would take over as memories of his cruelty, gaslighting, and lack of empathy resurfaced. How could she have been so blind? The guilt and embarrassment of being trapped in an abusive relationship for so long consumed her. She felt so stupid and unworthy. In her darkest moments, suicidal thoughts started creeping in, feeling that it was the only way to escape the pain.

Looking back now, she understands how normal and common it is to experience such turbulent and extreme emotions after leaving a narcissistic relationship. The manipulation and mind games they put you through make you question your own reality and self-worth.

# Mixed Emotions

Leaving a narcissistic partner is an incredibly difficult and emotional experience. One minute, you feel empowered and confident that you made the right choice to walk away from the abuse and toxicity. But then the mixed emotions start, making you question your decision. Suddenly, you're confused, believing things may have worked out if only you tried harder. The self-doubt and regret can be overwhelming.

This whirlwind of emotions can be isolating. As the narcissist typically cuts you off from friends and family over time, you may now find your support system has dwindled.

Some days, you'll be gripped by numbness, unable to fully process what you've been through. Other times, waves of anger will wash over you as memories of the gaslighting, cruelty, and your former partner's lack of empathy resurface. The injustice of it all can make you furious.

You may feel guilty and embarrassed for staying as long as you did. These feelings of unworthiness can be exacerbated by the narcissist's brainwashing tactics that made you believe you were the problem.

Turbulent and extreme emotions are completely normal and to be expected when leaving a narcissist. You've endured psychological torture and your emotions and self-esteem have been beaten down. It will take time to rebuild your sense of self and identity.

Remind yourself that this emotional turmoil is just temporary. You've been through an incredibly traumatic experience: Of course, there will be aftershocks as you begin to pick up the pieces and rebuild your life and identity.

Have confidence that with time and distance from the narcissistic abuse, you will start to heal. The self-doubt, guilt, and negative feelings about yourself will gradually go away. The explosive anger and mood swings will level out. You'll stop questioning your reality and recognize just how unacceptable and abusive the narcissist's behavior was.

# Effects of Narcissistic Abuse on the Children

Growing up with a narcissistic parent can affect a child's sense of self-worth and emotional well-being. When your parent is incapable of truly loving you for who you are, it sets you up for some serious struggles, both in childhood as well as adulthood.

From a young age, the narcissistic parent makes the child feel unloved and unworthy no matter how hard they try to please that parent. It's a constant stream of criticism, put-downs, and being told directly or indirectly that they're not good enough. As that message is hammered in year after year, it depletes the child's self-esteem. They start internalizing and believing the negative things said about them.

Living in that kind of toxic environment induces a chronic state of anxiety and hypervigilance fearing they'll do something wrong and trigger the next outburst or punishment from the narcissistic parent. The unpredictability and emotional manipulation really mess with their mental health, often leading to depression, anxiety disorders, and more issues down the line.

Children raised by narcissists also learn that love and approval must be earned through obedience and perfectionism. They develop people-pleasing, codependent tendencies, never feeling safe or free to be themselves. Their personal boundaries and autonomy are trampled on completely.

This makes it extremely difficult for them to develop a solid sense of self-identity. Who are they allowed to be, other than an extension of that parent's wants and demands? Their authentic self doesn't get a chance to develop.

As they get older, forming healthy relationships becomes an immense challenge. Having been deprived of that core secure attachment and trust from childhood, it's hard for them to open up and create intimacy. They may even subconsciously model the dysfunctional relationship patterns they learned growing up.

It's a cruel paradox really, as the people supposed to unconditionally love and nurture their children are the ones systematically chipping away at their sense of self-worth and emotional well-being through abuse and manipulation. These childhood wounds can be healed, but it takes a lot of work and commitment.

## The Narcissist Playing Victim to Their Children

Narcissistic parents are masters at playing the victim to manipulate their children's empathy and loyalty. They'll guilt trip the children into believing they're the victim, even though their own behavior is abusive.

For example, a narcissistic mother might lash out and scream demeaning insults at her teenage daughter over a small slight like leaving a dish in the sink. When the daughter gets upset and sets boundaries, the mom immediately turns it around: "After everything I've sacrificed to give you a good life, how can you treat me so disrespectfully? I'm just trying to teach you responsibility, but you make me out to be the bad guy, as usual."

She will paint herself as the selfless martyr mother whose thankless efforts are constantly dismissed by her ungrateful, cruel child. The daughter is suddenly ashamed and feels guilty. The child is trapped in consoling her "victim" parent.

This dynamic is reinforced any time the children express disagreement. The narcissist immediately goes into self-victimization mode: "You're ganging up on me." "Nothing I ever do is good enough for you two." "I'm such a horrible father, maybe you'd be better off without me." This histrionic behavior forces the kids to anxiously backpedal and reassure the fragile parent that they didn't mean to upset them.

The narcissist's persona of the long-suffering, misunderstood, unappreciated victim persists despite them often being the instigator and source of conflict. They are masters at deflecting any accountability by making their children's existence the sad burden they have no choice but to shoulder. They might even tell the children that they never wanted them, or that having children was one of the biggest mistakes they made.

From a young age, children naturally have a strong desire to please their parents and make them happy. This is a normal part of their emotional development and ability to empathize with others. However, a narcissistic parent can harmfully exploit this tendency.

Imagine a child who comes home from school feeling upset about something that happened. Instead of listening to the child's feelings and providing comfort, the narcissistic parent tells them they're being inconsiderate by complaining about their school since the parent works hard to provide for them and pay the school fees. In this scenario the parent now becomes the victim, while the child feels even worse, as they feel ashamed and guilty about their initial feelings, and also about how they treated their parent. The child may stop expressing their emotions so as to prioritize the parent's feelings.

The parent's self-victimization becomes a way to maintain control over the relationship and ensure that the child's boundaries and emotional reality are disregarded.

The narcissistic parent is using the child's empathy as a weapon by gaslighting them into believing that their feelings and needs are invalid or less important than the parent's. This can have long-lasting, negative impacts on the child's ability to form healthy relationships and maintain appropriate boundaries as they grow older.

## Helping Your Child Deal With the Narcissistic Parent

It can be difficult and unpleasant for children to have to deal with a narcissistic co-parent. However, you can do certain things to create a safe environment for them to process the dysfunction and develop a strong, healthy sense of self.

### Set Boundaries on Behalf of the Children

Enforce firm boundaries. Don't bend over backward trying to please them or avoid conflict—it never works and just makes it easier for them to behave in toxic ways. Lay out clear rules about unacceptable conduct and stick to them consistently. For example, you could say "I understand you're upset, but speaking to me or the children that way with insults and yelling is not okay. I'm happy to discuss this calmly later." This also models healthy behavior for your children.

## Safe Space at Your Home

Make your own home an oasis amidst the narcissistic chaos. Reinforce that your children don't have to tolerate disrespect, even from a parent. Reassure them that the hot/cold, demeaning, manipulative behavior they see is not their fault nor is it normal or acceptable—they deserve better. Let them freely express any anger, sadness, or confusion in a supportive environment. This allows them to process those feelings constructively and see that a healthier dynamic exists. However, don't negatively talk to them about their other parent.

### Being a Consistent, Loving Parent

Narcissists are notoriously unreliable and their moods shift wildly based on their desire for admiration. Do your best to be the stable, emotionally available parent who offers your children unconditional love, nurturing, and support. For example, if your ex was particularly cruel one visit, you could say "I know seeing mom get so angry and say hurtful things was really upsetting. Just remember, her struggles have nothing to do with what an amazing kid you are. I'm here for you always." This teaches them what a caring, stable parent-child relationship looks like.

### Outside Support System

It can help your kids emotionally if they have access to other caring adults outside of the narcissistic co-parent. Whether it's close relatives, teachers, counselors, or coaches, having positive role models and support systems they can turn to makes an immense difference in their lives.

For example, you could foster a close relationship with your parents and ensure they get regular quality time with their grandkids. Or you could get them involved with a Big Brothers Big Sisters program to have another dependable mentor in their life. Finding outlets outside of the narcissist's toxic presence is important.

## Professional Help

If you notice any concerning behavioral changes like anxiety, withdrawal, aggression, angry outbursts, or low self-esteem, don't hesitate to get your child into counseling. Having an objective professional help them process and unpack the narcissistic abuse and emotional neglect can be an invaluable tool for prevention. Their psychological needs must take priority over anything else.

It's a tough situation, but focusing your efforts on creating a secure, loving environment and providing the emotional support and guidance children of narcissists so desperately need can go a long way. They can become self-confident adults if they get the right support.

# Learning to Process Your Emotions and Emotional Regulation

Emotional regulation is a vital skill for recovering from a relationship with a narcissist. It involves managing and responding to your emotions in a healthy, constructive way. When you're able to regulate your emotions effectively, you can cope with the intense feelings that often arise after narcissistic abuse, set better boundaries, validate your own experiences, and build resilience for the challenges of the healing process.

First off, emotional regulation can help you manage those intense, painful feelings that often come up after a toxic relationship. Instead of getting swept away by anger, sadness, or fear, you can learn techniques to ground yourself and find a sense of calm. This might mean practicing deep breathing, mindfulness, or progressive muscle relaxation when stressed.

Emotional regulation also helps you set better boundaries. When you can recognize and manage your emotions, it's easier to communicate your needs assertively and stand up for yourself.

Another key aspect of emotional regulation is learning to validate your feelings. After being with a narcissist who constantly diminished or dismissed your emotions, you may start to doubt yourself. But by practicing self-compassion and reminding yourself that your feelings are valid, you can begin to trust your own instincts again.

Lastly, emotional regulation is all about developing resilience. When you have the tools to healthily cope with difficult emotions, you're better equipped to handle the ups and downs of the healing process. Instead of getting derailed by setbacks or triggers, you can keep moving forward on your journey toward recovery.

# Activity: Create a Feelings Wheel

This activity will help you better identify, understand, and process their emotions.

## *Materials*

- blank paper or printable feelings wheel template
- colored pens, pencils, or markers
- a quiet, comfortable space

## *Instructions*

1. Find a quiet place where you can do the activity without being distracted.

2. Take a blank piece of paper and draw a large circle in the center. You can also use a printable feelings wheel if you can find one online.

3. Divide the circle into six to eight sections, each representing a primary emotion such as anger, sadness, fear, joy, love, surprise, or disgust.

4. Create smaller sections or "spokes" for related secondary emotions within each primary emotion section. For example, under "anger," you might include frustration, irritation, resentment, and bitterness.

5. Using colored pens or markers, fill in each section with the appropriate emotion. Feel free to use colors that resonate with each emotion for you.

6. Once your feelings wheel is complete, take time to think about your current emotional state. Identify which primary and secondary emotions you're experiencing and locate them on your wheel.

7. Write down any thoughts, experiences, or triggers associated with these emotions. Explore how they relate to your past relationship with the narcissist and your current healing journey.

8. Consider sharing your feelings wheel and reflections with a trusted friend, family member, or therapist. Talking through your emotions can provide you with valuable insight and support.

9. Keep your feelings wheel in a safe, accessible place. Use it as a tool for daily check-ins or whenever you need to process complex emotions.

After you've completed the feelings wheel activity, take a moment to reflect on your experience. Consider the following questions:

- What emotions did you identify during the activity? Did any of them surprise you?

- How did it feel to name and visualize your emotions in this way?

- What did you learn about your emotional patterns and triggers?

- How could you use this tool to support your ongoing healing and emotional regulation?

Processing emotions after a narcissistic relationship is a complex, ongoing journey. Be patient and compassionate with yourself as you continue to explore and understand your feelings. With time and practice, activities like the feelings wheel can help you develop greater emotional awareness and resilience.

# Key Takeaways

- Leaving a narcissistic partner may cause many mixed emotions, including relief, doubt, confusion, isolation, anger, guilt, and embarrassment.

- These turbulent emotions are normal after enduring narcissistic abuse, which can damage self-esteem and your sense of reality. It will take time to heal.

- Children of narcissistic parents often struggle with low self-worth, anxiety, depression, and people-pleasing tendencies, and they may struggle to form healthy relationships as adults.

- Narcissistic parents play the victim to manipulate their children's empathy and maintain control, disregarding the child's feelings and boundaries.

- To help children deal with a narcissistic co-parent, set firm boundaries, provide a safe space for them to express their feelings, be a stable loving presence, ensure outside support, and get professional help if needed.

- Emotional regulation is key for healing from narcissistic abuse. It involves managing intense feelings, setting boundaries, validating your emotions, and building resilience.

In Chapter 3, we're going to look at how you can set boundaries to protect yourself and your children from narcissistic abuse.

# Chapter 3:

# Set Boundaries

Amy took a steadying breath as she heard the familiar sound of her ex-husband's car pulling into the driveway. It was Luke's scheduled time to pick up their children for the weekend. Just the thought of interacting with him made Amy's chest tighten with dread.

It'd been nearly a year since their divorce was finalized, but Luke could still make her question her reality with his mind games. The simplest exchange about parenting schedules or updates on the kids could incur spewed insults and projected blame, or dredge up agonizing memories of the emotional abuse that ended their marriage.

Taking a deep breath, Amy reminded herself of the personal boundaries she worked so hard to reinforce. She wouldn't tolerate Luke's toxic presence in her life or allow him to sabotage her healing. He was no longer welcome in her home unless the visit directly concerned the children's well-being.

Amy opened the door, ready to steer the conversation toward child-focused topics. Her ex was smirking as she opened the door, but she continued to give him the children's schedule for the weekend and talked to him about school updates.

Luke then started complaining and ranting about her "ways" as usual. However, Amy told him that she wouldn't be treated disrespectfully and that they could continue their conversation at another time. When he launched into a hysterical tantrum, she pressed her phone's recording app to record his tirade as evidence of his instability.

As the episode continued she walked back inside and locked the door on his raging without a second thought. She was proud of herself for standing up for her personal boundaries. This was just another step towards fully reclaiming her power and autonomy as a parent, despite her ex's efforts to erode it.

# Setting Boundaries

Setting boundaries is crucial for your own well-being and healthy co-parenting with a narcissistic ex. If you don't set limits from the start of your co-parenting relationship, they will take advantage of you.

Your ex wants to be able to pull your strings and get an emotional reaction from you when they feel a need for control. If you argue with them, defend yourself, or sink to their level you're just giving them what they want.

When your ex inevitably crosses boundaries with insults, demands, or disrespect, only discuss logistics around the children. If this doesn't work, walk away.

Document all communications, including everything that was said and done. Meticulous records neutralize their gaslighting and protect you legally. It's up to you to be the voice of reason and fact.

It's hard work, but establishing and enforcing boundaries with your narcissistic ex is worth it for your family's healing and well-being.

## *Physical Boundaries*

Establishing clear physical boundaries with your narcissistic ex is so important. However, it's easier said than done, as they have a tendency to violate boundaries and cause self-doubt.

When it comes to your home, think of it as a sacred haven for you and your children—free from your ex's mind games and emotional manipulation. Your ex shouldn't be on your property or in your house unless it directly relates to co-parenting logistics and custody exchanges. You don't have to invite them in for any other reason.

Your home should be free from their toxic presence, so politely, but firmly deny any attempts to get inside. They may tell you they need to use your bathroom or that they've forgotten something at your house; Don't fall for this type of manipulation.

Your ex may also try guilting you into spending time together "for the kids' sake" or commenting on how you're depriving the children of family unity. However, you don't owe them that emotional intimacy anymore, especially if they've been abusive. If you try to fake it for the kids' benefit, it will only confuse and potentially traumatize them more in the long run.

Parallel parenting with clear boundaries models healthy co-parenting much better than pretending your ex is still part of an intact family unit. Children pick up on tension and negativity.

So be confident about enforcing these physical boundaries. Don't let your ex overstay their welcome or cause an uncomfortable situation at your own home. You and your kids need a drama-free safe space without their toxicity.

## *Emotional Boundaries*

When you've been wounded by narcissistic abuse, protecting your peace is your top priority—even if it feels uncomfortable at first. The narcissist will try to regain control over you, but you shouldn't feel bad about shutting those attempts down.

Let's say you have an infant son, and your ex shows up at your door unannounced, angry and ranting about some drama with his new partner. While in the past you might have tried to calm him down, for the sake of your and your child's healing, don't get involved.

Tell him you're not prepared to get involved and that you will be closing the door. Follow through with what you've told him, even if he tries to get a reaction from you by calling you names or pounding on the door as you walk away. You're breaking free from the cycle of abuse by refusing to reinforce his unacceptable behavior by giving him more attention.

Another tactic is to call you incessantly and complain about minor co-parenting issues. You don't have to put up with this behavior, as you don't owe him anything. Let the phone go to voicemail, or simply tell him you'll be happy to discuss logistics about your son at another time and hang up the phone.

You shouldn't see protecting yourself from toxic interactions as rude; it's simply self-preservation. The narcissist distorts reality and violates basic decency.

## *Personal Boundaries*

Your ex will probably try to convince you that keeping some level of "friendship" is better for co-parenting or just maintaining the peace. However, this is likely just a way of trying to get access to you.

Let's say your narcissistic ex periodically sends you messages that you should catch up as friends for the kids' sake or go out for coffee. This might seem harmless enough, but you probably know how their fake concern and friendship can quickly turn into put-downs and jealousy, alienating you from your loved ones. You don't have to give this person access to your personal life, as they forfeited that privilege when they abused you. You don't owe them intimate updates about anything happening in your life.

In fact, you want the narcissist to know as little as possible about what's going on with you because as soon as they get access to information, they can try to use it to gain power over you, manipulate you, or sabotage your personal growth.

It's not cruel to shut down their attempts to try and reintegrate themselves into your life—you're defending the identity and autonomy, and reclaiming your freedom. Declining their attempts at friendship is not mean-spirited, but simply a practical and sensible move.

The narcissist could try to guilt trip you by acting shocked and hurt that you've "suddenly become so cold". However, you're under no obligation to do anything for them.

## *Financial Boundaries*

If you are financially dependent on your narcissistic partner, or vice versa, you need a clear plan for separating your finances as soon as possible. Don't think you'll find a middle ground that works for both of you; the narcissist is only interested in maintaining control.

In an ideal scenario, you're able to cut all financial ties cleanly by separating your assets, closing joint accounts, and becoming fully self-supporting.

This might not be feasible depending on your situation, especially if you are a stay-at-home parent or haven't worked for a while.

Try not to compromise or bargain directly with the narcissist about support payments, asset splits, or future finances. You might have to deal with intimidation and even financial abuse. You may need a family law expert to help you sort out your family's financial needs.

If possible, refuse to provide financial data directly to your ex and communicate solely through attorneys. Narcissists are notorious for draining resources and hiding money. Allowing them even an inch of access can mean they'll only exploit you more down the road.

This can be the most difficult part of extricating yourself from this dysfunctional relationship. You have to be prepared for devious behavior, such as draining the kids' college funds, taking out sketchy loans in your name, and other ways of ruining you financially. That's why setting and guarding financial boundaries are so important.

# Emotional Enmeshment

Potential enmeshment is another reason to set strict boundaries with a narcissistic co-payment. So what is emotional enmeshment?

It refers to a dysfunctional relationship pattern where personal boundaries are poorly defined or don't exist between family members, typically a parent and child. In an emotionally enmeshed relationship, there is an excessive level of involvement, invasion of privacy, and blurring of roles.

Children can become enmeshed with the narcissistic parent, often insidiously. Imagine a parent constantly needing their child's attention, approval, and admiration. This parent might overshare inappropriate details about their personal life or talk to their child about marital and relationship problems. They might frequently complain or vent to the child about their own issues, burdening the child with adult emotional baggage.

The narcissistic parent sees the child more as an extension of themselves rather than a separate individual, so the child's roles, wants, and needs get blurred with their own. For example, the parent could expect the child to prioritize caring for their emotional needs above everything else—like being available to provide constant reassurance, compliments, or comfort whenever the parent demands it. The child then becomes a parent to their parent, instead of the opposite.

The narcissistic parent might also invade the child's privacy by prying into personal details or not letting the child have any independence. The child is made to feel guilty anytime they try to be their own person separate from the parent.

This enmeshment means the child's own identity, boundaries, and sense of self become muddled and stunted. Their emotional development suffers because they can't properly individuate from the narcissistic parent. It creates an unhealthy, merged sense of identity where the child's self-worth comes to excessively depend on keeping the narcissistic parent happy and attending to their needs at the expense of the child's own needs.

## Managing Enmeshment Between Your Child and the Co-parent

It can be difficult, but it's possible to manage enmeshment between a parent and child.

Firstly, boundaries need to be reinforced. Be very clear with your co-parent about what is and is not appropriate in terms of their interactions with the children. Set limits on oversharing personal details, burdening children with adult issues, or making excessive demands for attention/validation.

Be a secure base for your child. Provide them with a safe, secure home environment where they can be themselves without feeling guilty or obligated to the narcissistic parent. Remind them that their needs and feelings also matter.

Encourage your children to develop their individuality and cultivate interests, friends, and a sense of identity separate from the narcissistic parent. Validate their right to privacy and independence.

Refuse to discuss or get drawn into the narcissistic manipulation tactics used by your co-parent, especially in front of your child.

It's important to help your child develop confidence and self-worth not contingent on pleasing the narcissistic parent. Praise them for effort rather than conditional acceptance.

Don't be afraid to find support and consider family therapy or counseling to help your child process the dysfunctional dynamics and learn coping strategies.

# Dealing With a Difficult Co-parent

Co-parenting can be really hard, especially if you have an ex who doesn't respect boundaries or engages in manipulative, narcissistic behavior. If this is your situation, protecting yourself and staying focused on what's best for your kids is important.

If your ex brings up inappropriate topics, insults you, or tries to goad you into an argument that has nothing to do with the children, don't take the bait. Narcissists thrive on getting an emotional reaction from you—it feeds their ego. The calmer you remain, the less satisfaction they get.

Have a few simple phrases ready like "I'm not going to discuss that right now. Let's stay focused on [child's name]" or "We can continue this conversation another time when it can be fully focused on the kids." Stop interacting with them about anything that isn't directly child-related.

# Documentation Is Key

Documentation becomes your friend when dealing with conflict in a co-parenting situation. It's vital to record everything related to your co-parenting interactions and responsibilities:

- Write down every time they refuse to share information about the children, show up late for custody exchanges, or break the rules you've agreed to. Note dates, times, and what was said.

- Document the positive things you do as a parent—days you have the kids, activities/appointments you take them to, expenses you cover, etc.. This creates a record of your active parenting.

- Hold on to any texts/emails where they are uncooperative, insulting, or not acting in the kids' best interests.

The goal isn't to try to "win" against your ex but to create a protective paper trail in case you ever need it. Having factual documentation shows you're the rational party focused on co-parenting responsibly.

## Medium Chill and Grey Rock

It's important to find ways to protect your emotions and avoid getting caught up in their drama. Two strategies that can help are called "medium chill" and "grey rock."

Medium chill is all about staying calm and not letting the narcissist get under your skin. When they try to provoke you, keep your responses short and neutral. Don't show them that you're upset or angry. Use a flat voice and try not to show any strong emotions on your face. If they keep trying to start a fight, change the subject, or talk about something boring. And if they just don't stop, find an excuse to leave the conversation.

**Here's an example:**

Narcissist: "You're always so selfish! You never consider my feelings!"

Medium Chill Response: "I'm sorry you feel that way. Oh, by the way, did you hear about the new restaurant opening downtown?"

Grey rock is similar, but it's more about making yourself seem as uninteresting as possible to the narcissist, kind of like a plain, grey rock. When they try to talk to you, give short, dull answers. Don't share any personal details about your life that they could use against you later. Be careful about what you share on social media, even if you're no longer friends on a social platform, as the narcissist may have their family and friends still lurking on your pages.

When you're around the narcissist, act like you don't have any strong feelings or opinions. Keep a straight face and don't show any excitement or anger.

**Here's an example:**

Narcissist: "What have you been up to lately? I bet you're still hanging out with those loser friends of yours."

Grey Rock Response: "Not much, just the usual. Work mostly."

Using these techniques can help you protect your emotional well-being and avoid getting sucked into pointless arguments with narcissists. They might feel weird at first, but they are useful tools for setting boundaries and avoiding manipulation.

## *Be the Steady, Child-Focused Parent*

As hard as it is when your ex is manipulative and crosses boundaries, do your best to stay calm and keep conversations focused on your children's needs. Kids need at least one steady, safe parent they can rely on amid any household tensions.

With consistent boundaries, documentation, and deferment of any emotional drama, you take away the narcissist's ability to gaslight or manipulate you. It shows your children that you are the stable, child-focused parent—which is ultimately what matters most.

# Activity: Setting Boundaries With Your Narcissistic Ex

This activity aims to help you set healthy boundaries with your narcissistic ex-partner.

## Instructions

Identify the areas where you need to set boundaries with your narcissistic ex.

These could include

- communication (e.g., frequency, method, content)
- personal space and privacy
- interactions with shared friends or family
- co-parenting (if applicable)
- financial matters

For each area, define specific boundaries that you feel are necessary for your emotional well-being and personal growth. Write these boundaries down in clear, concise language.

## Example Boundaries

- "I will only communicate with my ex via email or text, and only regarding essential matters."
- "I will not discuss my personal life or new relationships with my ex."
- "I will not attend social gatherings where my ex is present."

Develop a plan for communicating these boundaries to your ex.

Consider the following:

- Choose a method of communication that feels safe and comfortable for you (e.g. email, letter, or with the support of a therapist or mediator).

- Use assertive, non-aggressive language that focuses on your needs and feelings rather than blaming or attacking your ex.

- Be prepared for potential resistance or pushback from your ex, and plan how you will respond in a way that maintains your boundaries.

- Roleplay the conversation with a friend, family member, or therapist to practice acting firm when challenged and responding to potential challenges.

Keep a journal to track your progress and any instances where your ex attempts to violate your boundaries. Write down your responses to the challenges you have to deal with.

You should review and adjust your boundaries regularly, considering your personal growth and changing circumstances.

# Key Takeaways

- Setting clear boundaries is crucial for your well-being and healthy co-parenting with a narcissistic ex.

- Don't argue, defend yourself, or get emotional—they want to create drama and control.

- When they cross boundaries, only discuss logistics about the children; otherwise, walk away.

- Meticulously document all communications to neutralize gaslighting and protect yourself legally.

- Deny attempts for them to enter your home unless directly related to co-parenting logistics.

- Protect your emotional boundaries—don't engage with rants, drama, or constant phone calls.

- Shut down attempts to regain personal intimacy or "friendship"— you don't owe them access anymore.

- Get clear on financial boundaries and separation—don't try to compromise directly with them.

- Use attorneys to handle asset splits and child support to avoid exploitation and financial abuse.

- Stay calm and child-focused, and let documentation show you as the rational parent prioritizing the children.

In Chapter 4 we will look at how the narcissist can retaliate when you set boundaries, and what you can do about it.

# Chapter 4:

# The Backlash

Saanvi took a deep, steadying breath as she hit send on the text message informing her husband Arjun that she was filing for divorce. They had already been separated for a while, and Saanvi and her daughter were living in their own apartment. Her hands shook slightly from the adrenaline rushing through her veins. She was finally getting out after years of his mental abuse and control.

She didn't expect him to take the news gracefully and was prepared for angry retaliation. However, she had finally reached her limit living under his dark cloud of manipulation.

Sure enough, within hours the smear campaign began. Saanvi's phone flooded with vicious texts and voicemails portraying her as an unstable, unfaithful liar unfit for custody of their young daughter Ishan. Fake social media accounts told of how cruel she was and how she had abandoned her husband.

Saanvi's first instinct was to defend herself, but she resisted, remembering this was Arjun's signature tactic to reinitiate engagement and regain a foothold in exploiting her emotions. She muted and blocked as much as she could, knowing defending her truth would only breathe more life into Arjun's smear campaign.

Arjun also tried to retaliate in other ways. Suddenly her car was booted for alleged unpaid parking tickets she knew nothing about. Letters from creditors arrived about credit cards maxed out in her name. It was all psychological warfare as he attempted to bleed her finances to reinforce his control.

Arjun switched his next campaign to hoovering. He sent her bouquets of marigolds with pleading poems asking for another chance. He promised her a fresh start if they could reconcile. Saanvi's heart hurt for the good times, but her mind was resolved to stay the course.

When parental alienation tactics began—Arjun keeping Ishan from her on visitation weekends or filling her mind with twisted lies about her selfishness—Saanvi hit her emotional low. But her support group's coaching helped her remain the grounded, nurturing mother, certain her daughter would eventually see through the narcissist's manipulation.

Saanvi documented every provocation and leaned on the encouragement from her support system. Some days were really difficult, but Arjun's smear campaign and punishment cycle slowly lost its power over her.

Eighteen excruciating months later, Saanvi could exhale when the divorce was finalized. Though periodic flare-ups occurred, Arjun's retaliation had fizzled out as he grew bored from her refusal to react.

## Why Do Narcissists Retaliate?

Narcissists often retaliate against boundaries because they are driven by an intense need for control to get their own way. That's why they might lash out.

When you've finally built up the courage to establish firm boundaries with the narcissist in your life, they could go into outrage mode and make it their mission to punish you for defying their perceived control.

Deep down, the narcissist has a brittle sense of self-worth that is dependent on being able to manipulate and dominate others. Any act of personal autonomy feels like a threat that must be eradicated at all costs. Boundaries are unacceptable roadblocks to their entitlement.

That's why narcissists tend to retaliate aggressively when you establish boundaries for your own well-being. In their fractured mindset, you're the one being abusive by neglecting your duty to keep feeding their ego. Your independence ignites their deepest fears of being worthless and exposed as a fraud.

Retaliation takes form in all sorts of toxic ways calculated to gaslight you into questioning your values. One of their cruelest tactics is the smear campaign—spinning outrageous lies about you, trying to turn others against you, and creating a false narrative where you're the unstable villain. Narcissists are such adept manipulators that many will believe their disinformation and bemoan how you've "changed."

You may find yourself stalked physically or digitally as they obsess over trying to find some "truth" to expose and punish you with. They could also attempt to financially abuse and control you by withholding money and resources until you fall back in line.

Think of their abusive behavior as a loud temper tantrum rooted in crippling insecurities and fears.

So as gut-wrenching as the narcissist's retaliation is, have faith that you're doing the right thing by prioritizing your healing. Their vile behavior isn't a reflection of your self-worth but a projection of their own.

# How Does the Narcissist Retaliate?

Narcissists are masters of retaliation. One of the main ways of retaliation is to start a smear campaign against you.

## *Smear Campaign*

The smear campaign involves spreading false stories about you to make you look like the bad guy. Most narcissists unfortunately are so skilled at manipulation that people tend to believe them.

Even your friends may buy into the narcissist's twisted version of reality. It's difficult, but don't react or try to defend yourself. You know the truth about what really happened. No matter how convincing the narcissist's tales are, the facts haven't changed.

It's tempting to correct the record and prove your side of things. But arguing hardly ever works with a narcissist—they'll just twist it further. The best approach is to stay calm, and not engage in any smear campaign drama. The truth will come out eventually to those who matter. By not reacting, they don't have any power over you.

## *Stalking*

A narcissist can also retaliate through stalking. This involves obsessively tracking and watching every move, in-person or online.

If your ex is stalking you physically, they may show up unexpectedly wherever you go—your home, work, friends' houses, etc. They want to make you feel like you have no privacy or sense of safety. The constant feeling of being watched can make you afraid to leave your home.

They can also violate you through online stalking. The narcissist will pore over every single thing you post on social media, looking for any tiny detail they can twist and use against you. This can make you scared to share anything personal online for fear of how they may weaponize that information.

The narcissist's goal when stalking is to maintain control through fear. They want you to be paranoid and feel like you can never fully escape their reach, no matter how much distance you try to put between you.

If you're being stalked, take a break from social media to give you some emotional breathing room. When it comes to a physical stalker, take extra safety precautions like changing your routes, getting a security system, or even moving to another area.

As difficult as it is, try not to engage or respond to the stalking—that's just giving the narcissist the reaction they crave. With time and boundaries, the obsessive behavior should subside.

## *Financial Abuse*

The narcissist may use money as a weapon to punish or reward certain behaviors. Narcissists can behave in peculiar ways when money is involved.

For example, if you have an interaction that pleases the narcissist, they may "reward" you with some cash or pay a bill they owe. But if you defy them or set boundaries, they'll withhold anything they're obligated to provide financially—like child support or alimony.

The narcissist does this to make you dependent on their goodwill and afraid to disagree with them, as you then risk losing financial support. It's a sick means of forcing compliance, even after the actual relationship has ended.

That's why it's so important when divorcing or leaving a narcissistic partner to get iron-clad financial agreements and court orders in place. Don't leave any room for them to conveniently "forget" or willfully refuse to pay what they owe as punishment. Establishing firm financial boundaries removes that leverage the narcissist once held over you.

It's also wise to work towards complete financial independence so you're not relying on the narcissist's contributions. That may mean getting on a tight budget, going back to work, or crashing with family for a while. It's not easy, but it's better than staying trapped in the narcissist's sick game of damaging financial abuse.

## *Weaponized Incompetence*

Weaponized incompetence refers to someone deliberately performing tasks poorly or claiming they are unable to accomplish something as a way to manipulate a situation to their advantage. A narcissist uses this tactic to avoid responsibilities, undermine their partner's confidence, maintain control, or punish their partner.

While you were still together, the narcissist may have conveniently forgotten to do chores or household tasks that you had asked them to do. They make it seem like they are simply incompetent at these things, forcing you to do it yourself or nag at them repeatedly if you want the task done. Now that you're no longer together, they may conveniently "forget" to buy the children the clothes or school supplies you had asked them to until you nag them about it. This gives the narcissist power as they control their partner's effort and attention.

It's challenging to deal with this type of behavior from your ex, but there are ways in which you can:

- Firstly, you have to set clear boundaries and expectations. Communicate your needs directly and inform them of the consequences if they are not met. Make it clear that it will not be to their advantage if they don't meet reasonable requests.

- Stop enabling the behavior. Do not do tasks for them or clean up after their "incompetence." This will just make them believe that they can get away with their dysfunctional behavior.

- When they claim they're unable to do something, call them out calmly. Tell them that you know they're capable of doing something and expect them to take care of it.

- Follow through on consequences. If they refuse to fulfill obligations, calmly enforce repercussions, for example, contacting their lawyer.

- Don't get involved in an argument with the narcissist, as it is never-ending.

- Take breaks from them as their behavior can be emotionally draining. Use positive self-talk, and remind yourself their actions aren't a reflection of your worth.

## *Baiting*

While ending a toxic relationship with a narcissist can be extremely difficult, becoming involved in retaliatory mind games isn't healthy for anyone involved. It can actually keep the cycle of abuse going and prevents you from healing and moving forward.

Disengage from the narcissist as much as possible, avoid taking the bait to become involved in their dramas, set firm boundaries about what behaviors you will not accept, and seek support from loved ones or a therapist if needed. Responding with compassion while protecting yourself can help you break the patterns of toxicity.

## Flying Monkeys

"Flying monkeys" is an expression used to describe people whom a narcissist or abusive person may subconsciously or consciously recruit to do their bidding and enable toxic behaviors.

In the context of a narcissistic relationship or following a breakup, "flying monkeys" might refer to the narcissist's friends or family members whom they have turned against you through lies, manipulation, or false stories and lies. These people may then act as additional instruments of the narcissist's abuse by attacking you, passing along insults or disinformation, or pressuring you to comply with the narcissist's demands.

So how do you deal with these flying monkeys?

Communicate your boundaries clearly and let them know what the consequences will be if they cross them. You don't have to put up with their bad behavior, and it's up to you to let them know what's acceptable.

Reduce or eliminate your contact with flying monkeys. This makes it less likely for their behavior to affect you, and it also prevents them from gathering information that they can give to the narcissist.

If they have provoked you, don't react emotionally. Flying monkeys usually try to get a strong reaction that can be used against you.

You can try to explain your side of the story to the flying monkeys, as they may be acting based on manipulation or misinformation. However, be prepared that they may not be open to understanding if they have been too deeply manipulated.

Finally, keep records of your interaction with flying monkeys. This can be especially useful if you have to provide evidence of manipulation or harassment.

## Hoovering

Your ex could use hoovering tactics to try and pull you back into their life. The term "hoovering" suggests they are trying to "suck" you back into the relationship. This manipulation can show up in different ways, like suddenly reaching out, making big promises to change, or showering you with compliments and gifts. They might also play the victim, trying to make you feel sorry for them, or create fake emergencies to get your attention.

It's important to understand that hoovering is a way to regain control and not a genuine change of heart. Set firm boundaries and stick to them. If possible, cut off all communication. Block their number and avoid them on social media. If you can't completely avoid contact, like in co-parenting situations, try the grey rock method—be as dull and unresponsive as possible.

## *Parental Alienation*

Parental alienation is a form of psychological manipulation where one parent attempts to turn the child against the other parent. It's quite common in a divorce or separation from a narcissist.

Some common alienating behaviors include

- bad-mouthing or portraying the other parent as unfit, unloving, or dangerous to the child without legitimate cause
- limiting contact between the child and the targeted parent
- forcing the child to reject the other parent's values and feelings
- creating the impression the other parent abandoned the child

The effects on children can be extremely damaging—low self-esteem, guilt, depression, anxiety, and strained ability to form healthy relationships later on.

Fighting alienation is really tough, but there are things that can help:

- Keep careful records of every incident when it happens and keep the proof.
- Don't stoop to the same level. Be the calm, loving, stable parent.
- Get a therapist involved to help rebuild the bond with your child.
- Use tools like co-parenting apps to communicate clearly without room for misunderstandings.

- If nothing else works, you may need to take legal action to enforce the court-ordered parenting time.

The most important thing is to protect the well-being of your children.

## Disneyland Parenting

Disneyland parenting is a term used to describe a narcissistic parenting style where parents try to be their child's best friend instead of a responsible authority figure. Everything needs to be fun and exciting for the child, like a trip to Disneyland, without setting appropriate boundaries or expectations.

Here are some key characteristics of Disneyland parenting:

- These parents avoid setting rules or enforcing consequences because they don't want to be the "bad guy" or upset their child. They would rather give in to the child's demands than deal with tantrums or disagreements.

- They spoil their child with excessive gifts, treats, and experiences, often out of a desire to be loved or seen as the "cool" parent. They may also use material items to compensate for a lack of emotional connection.

- They treat their child as if they can do no wrong and constantly praise them, even for small or insignificant things. This can lead to an inflated sense of self-importance in the child.

- They share too much personal information with their child or involve them in adult matters. They may also rely on the child for emotional support or companionship in an inappropriate way. This leads to the parentification of the child, as they may also lean on their children for emotional support.

- Their parenting style can be unpredictable and inconsistent, with rules and expectations changing based on their mood or the child's demands.

While it's natural for parents to want their children to be happy, Disneyland parenting can have negative consequences. Children raised in this environment will struggle with self-control, entitlement, and a lack of resilience when faced with challenges or disappointments. They also struggle to form healthy relationships or take responsibility for their actions.

It can be difficult to co-parent with a Disneyland parent. They could undermine your authority by disregarding or mocking the rules and boundaries you try to set for the children when they are with you. This creates inconsistency and confusion for the kids.

They spoil the kids with excessive gifts, junk food, late nights, etc. when they have them, attempting to position themselves as the "cool" parent the kids prefer. When the kids stay with you, you may struggle to keep them in their routine or meet their daily obligations such as doing homework.

The narcissist could also bad-mouth you to the children. They may speak negatively about you to the kids or blame you for disciplining them or saying no. They could even try to turn the children against you by saying you don't love them if you enforce rules or boundaries.

The Disneyland parent creates an unstable inconsistent environment by switching between homes. Staying calm and sticking to your own healthy boundaries is important while avoiding fighting in front of the kids.

# Activity: Developing Strategies to Deal With Narcissists and Their Flying Monkeys

The aim is to help you develop a plan for interacting with the narcissist and their flying monkeys (enablers or supporters) while protecting your emotional well-being.

### *Instructions*

Identify the narcissists and flying monkeys in your life. Make a list of these people and their roles in supporting the narcissist's behavior.

For each person on your list, describe the types of manipulative or enabling behaviors they exhibit. These may include

- gaslighting or denying the narcissist's abusive behavior
- defending or justifying the narcissist's actions
- pressuring you to forgive or reconcile with the narcissist
- spreading gossip or misinformation about you on behalf of the narcissist

Decide how you want to deal with them, by thinking about the following options:

- Only have limited or no contact with the flying monkeys if you feel they're bad for your well-being.
- Set boundaries for acceptable behavior and topics of discussion.
- Use medium chill or grey rock techniques to minimize emotional reactivity and avoid fueling conflicts.
- Seek support from trusted friends, family members, or a therapist to validate your experiences and maintain perspective.

### Example Strategy

Flying monkey: Your sibling pressures you to reconcile with the narcissistic parent.

Boundary: "I understand that you want us to have a united family, but I need to prioritize my own well-being. I ask that you respect my decision to limit contact with Mom, even if you don't agree with it."

# Key Takeaways

Narcissists use the following retaliation tactics:

- Smear campaigns: spreading lies and disinformation to turn others against you

- Stalking: obsessively tracking your movements, online or in-person

- Financial abuse: withholding money/resources as punishment

- Weaponized incompetence: deliberately doing tasks poorly to undermine you

- Baiting: trying to provoke reactions and drag you into dramas

- Flying monkeys: recruits who enable the narcissist's toxic behaviors

- Hoovering: love-bombing to try and suck you back into the relationship

- Parental alienation: manipulating children to reject the other parent

- Disneyland parenting: overindulging children to be the "cool" friend-parent

In Chapter 5, we'll look at the benefits of having a parenting plan.

# Chapter 5:

# Create a Parenting Plan

The flashing digital numbers on the microwave read 6:17 p.m.. Emma paced back and forth in the kitchen, phone gripped tightly in her hand as she waited for Doug's call or text saying he was on his way. Their custody agreement clearly stated Friday pickups were at 6 p.m. sharp. If he was more than 30 minutes late without proper notice, the children had to stay with her for the weekend.

At 6:23 p.m., her phone buzzed. "Running late, be there by 7:30," Doug's message read. Emma felt her blood pressure rise. This was the third time in two months he had blown off the agreed pickup time with no valid excuse, meaning she also had to change her plans.

She replied, "As per our agreement if you don't arrive by 6:30 p.m. the kids stay with me this weekend. We can't keep doing this casual back-and-forth, it's not fair to them."

Her children looked at her with worried eyes, sensing the tension. Emma managed a reassuring smile, but her stomach was in knots. With Doug, even the simplest plan could collapse into a huge power struggle.

At 6:42 p.m., her ex-husband's car pulled up with a screech of tires. Emma took a deep breath and gathered the kids' backpacks. As Doug stormed up the front walk, she reminded herself to stay calm and stick to the facts. Having an ironclad co-parenting plan with explicit rules was her only protection against his manipulation tactics.

"What's your problem?" Doug snapped as Emma opened the door. "The kids were ready, I'm not even that late."

"Our agreement says pickup is at 6 p.m., you didn't get here until 6:42 p.m.," she replied. "That's past the 30-minute grace period, so per the guidelines, the kids stay with me this weekend."

It was as if she'd slapped him. Doug's eyes burned with rage.

Living and co-parenting with a narcissist requires airtight boundaries and rules to prevent their mind games from controlling your life. If you have a self-centered ex who is constantly breaking the rules, it's important to have clear agreements and consequences for the sake of your sanity. When you don't give them leeway to manipulate you, they have less power to wreak havoc on you and your children.

# What Is a Parenting Plan and Why Do You Need It

A parenting plan is a formal written document that lays out the specific custody schedule, visitation details, and rules around how you will co-parent your children after a separation or divorce. It's an official guideline that both parents must follow.

If you are co-parenting with a narcissistic ex, having a detailed and airtight parenting plan is absolutely crucial. Here's why:

- It removes ambiguity and gray areas that a narcissist will exploit. Narcissists thrive on chaos, confusion, and being able to bend the rules for their own benefit. A clear parenting plan eliminates that.

- It holds the narcissistic parent accountable. You can point to the plan as the authority, rather than having a narcissist try to manipulate or gaslight you about what the "rules" are.

- It helps protect your children from instability. With dates, times, and responsibilities spelled out explicitly, it sets structure that narcissists often lack.

- It reduces conflict. Clearly defined terms cut down on the petty disagreements and power struggles a narcissist loves to engage in. You can refer back to the plan.

- It gives you legal leverage if issues arise. Having an official court-approved plan lets you take violations more seriously and you can take legal action if need be.

The parenting plan needs to spell out even the smallest details like the following:

- specific custody schedule with start/end days and times
- holiday/vacation scheduling
- drop-off and pickup locations
- what happens if a parent is late for their time
- how other caregivers or vacations with kids must be approved
- what decisions each parent can make unilaterally
- methods of communication between parents
- who is responsible for what costs

The more detailed, the better. Narcissists are masters at twisting any tiny gray area or miscommunication for their benefit. An ironclad parenting plan protects you and your children. While it's not a perfect solution, it does remove many opportunities for a narcissist's mind games and manipulation.

# Example Parenting Plan

You can use the following example to create your own parenting plan.

## *Co-parenting Plan With [Name]*

### *Communication*

All communication regarding the children should be done through a co-parenting app (e.g. OurFamilyWizard, TalkingParents) or email to maintain a written record.

Communication should be limited to matters concerning the children and respectful and free from insults, accusations, or derogatory language.

## Decision-Making

Major decisions regarding the children's education, healthcare, and general well-being should be jointly made by both parents.

If you disagree, you will seek mediation or consult a third-party professional such as a psychologist or counselor for guidance.

## Parenting Time

The children will spend alternating weekends and one weekday evening with each parent, as outlined in the schedule.

Exchanges will occur at a neutral location (e.g. school, public library) or through a third-party service if necessary.

Each parent will respect the other's parenting time and avoid disruptions or unannounced visits.

## Financial Responsibilities

Both parents will contribute to the children's expenses (e.g. medical, educational, extracurricular activities) according to their respective incomes.

A detailed record of expenses and contributions needs to be kept.

## Conflict Resolution

When there is a conflict or disagreement, both parents will commit to resolving issues through mediation or counseling before involving the court.

As parents, don't involve the children in adult disputes or attempt to alienate them from the other parent.

## Flexibility and Modifications

This co-parenting plan can be modified as needed, provided both parents agree to the changes.

Regular reviews (yearly or twice a year) will be scheduled to determine how effective the plan is and if it needs to be adjusted.

## Contingency Plan

In the event of an emergency or unforeseen circumstance, both parents will prioritize the children's safety and well-being.

A backup plan (e.g. temporary caregiver, emergency contacts) should be devised for emergencies.

Remember, when co-parenting with a narcissist, it's essential to maintain firm boundaries, document all interactions, and seek professional support such as counseling and mediation when you need it.

# On Vacation With the Narcissistic Parent

Going on vacation with a narcissistic co-parent can be an anxiety-filled experience with all kinds of problems.

A holiday together is usually an opportunity to create precious memories with your child; however, a narcissistic parent could sabotage the experience in all kinds of ways. For example, they could invite others without asking you, robbing the family of time they could have spent together. They could also make decisions about activities and accommodations without asking anyone else about their preferences.

## Vacation Parameters

If you and/or your children hope to make the best of a vacation with a narcissistic ex, have parameters explicitly outlined in your co-parenting plan.

Provide advance notice of the location and duration of the vacation and who will be attending. This can help you figure out in advance if there are any potential concerns, unsafe environments, or any of the narcissist's enabling family or friends who might be attending.

Clear guidelines also make it less likely that the narcissist will be able to control and manipulate situations during the holiday. If plans change suddenly or you discover they've invited others without your consent, you can refer back to the terms agreed on as a guideline to set boundaries.

Ultimately, having guidelines even for vacations helps to make the situation more predictable for your children. The child can make happy memories, even with the co-parenting challenges.

## No "Makeup" Days

When co-parenting with a narcissist, it's important to have clear rules around missed parenting time and communication. These boundaries help minimize power struggles and conflicts that can be so draining.

Let's say your ex is supposed to have your child for the weekend, but they cancel at the last minute because they made other plans. With a narcissist, simply making up that time on another day or weekend opens up a whole can of worms. They may try to demand extra days as "compensation." Before you know it, you're stuck in an endless cycle of arguing and keeping score.

If they miss their time, they should forfeit it with no makeup period. This will prevent them from turning the situation into a power play. It's frustrating, but you'll hopefully avoid more conflict down the road.

## Right of First Refusal and Notification Requirements

It's essential to have clear rules about childcare and your children's whereabouts. These types of boundaries help prevent your ex from playing games and pulling power moves that could be unhealthy or even unsafe for your child.

The right of first refusal is a smart guideline you can put in place. If either parent needs someone else to watch the children during their scheduled time—like a babysitter or family member—they legally have to offer that time to the other parent first before making other arrangements.

Let's say your narcissistic ex has your son this weekend, but then gets invited to some work function they want to attend. They can't just pass your son off to a friend or their new partner without letting you know first and giving you the chance to keep him instead. This helps maximize the time your child spends with the two people who matter most—their parents.

Maybe this sounds controlling, but remember that you're looking out for your kid's best interests. With a narcissist, you never know what kinds of unsavory characters or risky situations they might try to expose your child to otherwise. Giving you the right of first refusal means your child isn't exposed to unnecessary third parties.

### The Child's Whereabouts

It's also reasonable to request that your ex should share your child's whereabouts if they will be traveling a significant distance away, for example, a 50-mile radius.

For any overnight trips, even if it's a vacation during their time, you should get the details of where they'll be staying and for how long. This ensures that your child is safe and peace of mind. The narcissist will always prioritize themselves, and you don't want your child to be dragged into sketchy situations.

If you know where your child is at all times, you can step in if you don't trust the situation.

These boundaries could seem strange to someone who is co-parenting with a caring, reasonable person, but they're absolutely necessary when dealing with a narcissist's self-absorption and lack of judgment. Your child's well-being has to come before your ex's feelings or warped sense of control.

Setting these guidelines and critically enforcing them shows the narcissist that you won't bend to their manipulation. It creates stability and transparency in a chaotic situation. At the end of the day, your child needs a protective and loving parent.

# Other Legal Protections

There are some other protections you may want to consider if your ex is a difficult co-parent.

## *Custody and Visitation Order*

The narcissistic co-parent may feel entitled to call the shots about when they get to see the kids without respecting your time.

For example, say you and your ex had agreed that you'd have the kids on weekends. But then your ex starts saying, "Actually, I've decided to keep them this weekend because we have plans." Or they show up hours late for your visits without any excuse.

That's where getting an official custody and visitation order from the court can really help. The judge will review both parents' situations and spell out in a legally binding document exactly when each parent gets time with the kids.

So if the order says you get them every other weekend from Friday evening until Sunday evening, your ex can't just decide to keep them that weekend because you have it in writing. The schedule has to be followed.

And if your ex purposefully violates that schedule repeatedly, you'll have legal grounds to take them back to court for enforcement because they are violating a court order.

Having official paperwork takes a lot of the control away from a narcissistic ex trying to call all the shots. It sets firm boundaries that they must respect when it comes to time with the kids.

## *Supervised Visitation*

Sometimes when there are major worries about a parent's behavior or ability to properly care for a child, the court may order that the parent can only spend time with the child if another adult is present to supervise the visits.

Imagine your ex has a habit of losing their temper and yelling or saying really hurtful things to you and the kids when they're upset. Or maybe things have even gotten physically aggressive or out of control. As a result, you're genuinely concerned about your child's emotional or physical safety when they're alone with your ex.

In cases like this, you can ask the judge to put in place supervised visitation for your ex. This means they don't get to be completely alone with the child during their scheduled parenting time. Instead, there has to be an approved third-party adult present at all times to monitor the visits and make sure the child is safe.

The supervisor is typically a professional from an agency, but could potentially be a mutual relative or friend that both parents agree on, as long as the court approves that person. Their role is to monitor the parent-child interactions, step in if anything gets out of hand, and look after the child's well-being during visits.

So while it does restrict the time that parent gets to spend completely alone with the child, it provides an added layer of protection when there are legitimate safety concerns due to a history of verbal, emotional, or physical mistreatment by the narcissistic parent.

## *Disparagement Order*

Imagine your ex has a bad habit of constantly bad-mouthing you in front of the kids. Every time you drop them off or pick them up, your ex starts ranting about what a terrible person and parent you are. They might call you hurtful names, exaggerate your flaws, or outright lie to turn the kids against you.

This is not only unfair to you, but it's also really confusing and upsetting for the kids to hear one parent trashing the other like that. It puts them in the middle of your conflicts in an unhealthy way.

A no-disparagement order can help manage this type of behavior. It means the court prohibits both parents from saying disparaging or alienating remarks about each other when the children are present or can overhear it.

When the order is in place, your ex can't call you names, make rude comments about your parenting abilities, or try to convince the kids that you're a bad or uninvolved parent, as this would violate the court order. It sets clear boundaries that adversity between parents needs to be handled away from the children. It protects the kids from toxic conflict and parental alienation.

## *Mental Health Provisions*

Sometimes when parents are going through a divorce or custody case, the judge may have concerns about one parent's mental health or ability to properly care for the children. This could be due to issues like anger problems, substance abuse, or narcissistic/abusive tendencies.

The judge can write into the official custody order a requirement that the parent attends certain types of counseling, therapy, or parenting classes before or during their parenting time.

For example, let's say your ex has a long history of flying into rages and yelling horrible things at you and the kids when they don't get their way. The court may order that your ex has to complete an anger management program and provide proof to the court before being granted unsupervised visitation.

Or if your ex constantly puts their own needs first and struggles with excessive entitlement issues that impact the kids, the judge can mandate that they attend regular individual therapy to work on changing their narcissistic patterns.

The reason for these requirements is to hopefully improve that parent's coping skills, emotional regulation, and overall ability to prioritize the children's well-being during their parenting time.

Your ex will be held accountable for getting the support and guidance they need to be a better, safer parent presence in their children's lives. Their custody time can be restricted or supervised if they don't comply with the mental health provisions.

## Child Support

When parents split up, one parent may try to use money to control the other parent and the children. This is common behavior from narcissistic exes.

For example, let's say you and your ex didn't have a formal child support order. Every month, they give you a different excuse about why they can't afford to pay the full amount you had agreed on for the kids' expenses. They had unforeseen expenses or hadn't been paid all the money they should have received.

Without a court order, you could find yourself in a situation where you have to negotiate and beg for the financial support you're owed. Your ex can keep dangling that carrot of child support as a way to make you comply with their demands.

If you get an official, legally binding child support order from the court, it takes that financial control away from the narcissist. The judge will calculate how much child support must be paid monthly based on both parents' incomes and situations.

That amount is now set in stone by the court order. Your ex can't decide not to pay it or shortchange you whenever they feel like it. If they fail to pay the court-ordered child support, you have legal options to enforce it, like garnishing their wages.

The same applies to other child-related expenses beyond just the monthly support payment. The court order can spell out how major costs like health care, child care, and extracurricular activities will be shared between the parents.

Having a court order stops your narcissistic ex from calling all the financial shots unfairly.

## *Emergency Orders*

Sometimes, things could turn ugly with a narcissistic ex. If your ex physically intimidates you, makes threats of violence, or acts in an overall scary and unstable way, you may need legal protection quickly. This is where emergency orders from the court can help keep you and your children safe. One option is to request a restraining order or order of protection against your ex.

With a restraining order, the court legally forbids your ex from any physical violence, harassment, stalking, or even contacting you in most cases. They have to keep their distance and are prohibited from coming near you, your home, your workplace, your kids' schools, and so on.

If they violate the restraining order, they face very serious legal consequences like fines or jail time. Having that official court order makes any threats or intimidation tactics a criminal offense.

Another option in high-risk situations is requesting an emergency custody order that suspends your ex's visitation rights or their parenting time temporarily. The court does this when there are legitimate fears for the children's safety around that parent until things can get sorted out.

So if your narcissistic ex has become unhinged and is making you feel unsafe through threats, abusive behavior, or seems potentially violent, you can take legal action right away. Don't wait for something terrible to happen first.

By getting an emergency restraining or custody order, you create court-mandated protections that limit what your ex can legally do. It's a way to forcibly establish firm boundaries when you feel endangered by their narcissistic rage or retaliation.

An attorney who understands high-conflict, narcissistic dynamics knows how to push for tailored provisions that truly constrain the narcissist's games. They create court orders the narcissist can't easily violate without legal percussions.

# Activity: Parenting Plan

Use the following checklist to help you create your parenting plan. Your plan should cover all the essential aspects of co-parenting. Use this list to ensure that everything has been included in your plan.

## Parenting Time Schedule

- ❑ regular weekly schedule
- ❑ holiday and vacation schedules
- ❑ special occasions (birthdays, Mother's/Father's Day, etc.)
- ❑ makeup time for missed visitations

## Exchange of the Children

- ❑ pickup and drop-off locations
- ❑ times for exchanges
- ❑ procedures for handling delays or cancellations

## Communication

- ❑ preferred method of communication between parents
- ❑ response time expectations
- ❑ guidelines for emergency situations
- ❑ communicating with the children during the other parent's time

## Decision-Making

- ❑ areas requiring joint decision-making (e.g. education, healthcare)
- ❑ process for making joint decisions
- ❑ procedure for resolving disagreements

## Child Support and Expenses

- ❑ child support payments (amount, frequency, method)
- ❑ additional expenses (e.g. extracurricular activities, school supplies)
- ❑ medical expenses and insurance coverage

## Parenting Guidelines

- ❑ consistent rules and discipline across households
- ❑ bedtimes and routines
- ❑ screen time and internet usage
- ❑ diet and nutrition

## Introducing New Partners

- ❑ guidelines for introducing new partners to the children
- ❑ expectations for partner involvement in parenting

## Modification and Review

- ❑ circumstances that warrant plan modifications
- ❑ schedule for reviewing and updating the plan

## Dispute Resolution

- ❑ process for resolving disagreements (e.g. mediation, counseling)
- ❑ consequences for non-compliance with the plan

## Special Considerations

- ❑ provisions for children with special needs
- ❑ religious or cultural considerations
- ❑ any other unique family circumstances

After you have completed the checklist, review the plan with the other parent and adjust it where needed.

# Key Takeaways

- A detailed and airtight parenting plan is important when co-parenting with a narcissistic ex.
- The parenting plan removes ambiguity and gray areas that a narcissist can exploit and holds them accountable as parents.
- A parenting plan establishes boundaries and enforcement to show you won't bend to the narcissist's manipulation.
- The plan also prioritizes the child's well-being over your ex's control.

In Chapter 6, we will look at how you can deal with high-conflict parenting.

# Chapter 6:

# The Tool Belt

Co-parenting with Jared was like an endless boxing match for Sarah. Just when she thought she had things under control, he would lash out with another jab, always aiming at her insecurities as a parent. She had to tiptoe through their communications as if she was walking through a minefield.

Jared constantly changed the schedules for pickups and drop-offs on a whim. He wanted to retain full control and make Sarah dance to his tune. One day, she arrived 15 minutes early for her scheduled pickup time as usual. Not only was Jared not ready, but he berated her in front of the kids for being "so eager to rip them away from me." When being passive didn't work, Sarah learned she couldn't engage. She stated she was sticking to scheduled times and would leave at the set time, documenting everything.

Jared would interrogate the kids about every little detail at Sarah's house—what they ate, what they watched, who she spent time with. Any tiny deviation became "proof" that she was an unfit parent. He wanted to make her feel incompetent so the kids would choose him as the main custodial parent. Jared would pull the kids aside and turn them against Sarah. When boundaries didn't work, she had to reaffirm to the kids that families can do things differently and that's okay. She worked on building their self-trust and confidence.

There were many times when Jared would withhold bringing the kids for Sarah's scheduled visits because he was "too busy" or would claim one of them was sick. After a while, it was clear it was just manipulation when they were perfectly fine on his social media posts. He punished Sarah by weaponizing the kids, knowing it was what would hurt her the most. When being the "bigger person" failed, Sarah may have had to get courts involved for orders of enforcement and penalties for violations.

Through all of Jared's mind games, Sarah had to keep reminding herself his behavior was a reflection of his own brokenness, not hers or the kids'.

Some days she handled it with grace, others not so much. However, she never gave up on being the protective, stable, and loving parent her children needed. No matter how many jabs Jared threw, she kept her guard up and her eye on what was really important—the emotional well-being of her children.

# What Is High-Conflict Parenting?

High-conflict parenting is co-parenting with someone unwilling to cooperate, communicate effectively, or put the children's best interests first.

Imagine you and your ex share custody of your two kids. On paper, you split time 50/50 and the schedule seems fair. In reality, dealing with your ex is like slogging through a battlefield every single week.

Simple things like drop-off and pickup become opportunities for conflict and drama. They constantly show up late or try to change the time at the last minute to inconvenience you. When you raise the issue calmly, they blow up and accuse you of being irrational or "taking away their time" with the kids.

Discussions about important issues like health care, education, or discipline are completely unproductive. Your ex twists everything into an argument, name-calling and attempting to undermine your parenting decisions and authority in front of the children. You worry it's creating instability for the kids.

Money is another major flashpoint. If you ask about covering expenses like sports fees or clothes, your ex instantly becomes evasive or starts interrogating you about how every single dollar gets spent on "your time." It's a fight about every single expense.

The worst is when your ex tries limiting your communication with the kids or keeping them from you out of spite. You might get home from work to cruel messages that the kids are "sick" or they make up a ridiculous reason why they can't come this weekend per the agreed schedule.

You can see the effect it has on the children—your son is acting out, and your daughter is becoming anxious. You feel powerless because your ex is relentless and unwilling to co-parent or compromise in any way for the kids' well-being. It's an endless cycle of putting out fires while trying to stay the sane, stable parent.

# Narcissistic Rage

Narcissistic rage can be scary and confusing, especially for kids. It's when a parent with a narcissistic personality explodes in intense anger over something that seems insignificant to others.

For example, you accidentally forgot to put your dish in the sink after a meal. For a regular person, no big deal—they might just remind you to do it next time. But a narcissist could fly into a terrifying fit of rage, yelling, cursing, calling you ungrateful or intentionally trying to disrespect them.

When narcissistic rage takes over, they can seem like a different person, at least temporarily. They lose all control and self-restraint, breaking things, slamming doors, or even getting physically aggressive. All their narcissistic insecurities get channeled into explosive anger.

And no matter how small the issue that set them off, they'll never take responsibility for overreacting. In their minds, it was the child's fault for provoking their rage in the first place. The child will be berated about how terrible of a child they are who never listens or follows rules. The cruel, devaluing words they say during these rages can really leave psychological scars.

For kids living with a narcissistic parent's frequent rages, it creates an extremely unsafe, unstable environment. They're always walking on eggshells, trying their best not to trigger the next explosive episode. They minimize their needs to placate the raging parent. Verbal abuse and put-downs chip away at their self-esteem over time

The rational parent must create a protective, calming space apart from the chaos and trauma of the rages. Don't try to engage or resolve things in that heated state—walk away if you can. Prioritize your child's emotional well-being by building up their self-esteem, reassuring them it's not their fault, and taking them to counseling if needed so that they can process these experiences healthily. Most importantly, model emotional regulation by setting firm boundaries about unacceptable explosive behavior.

## How to Deal With High-Conflict Parenting

Let's look at different examples of high-conflict parenting and how you can deal with them.

### Example 1: The Ex Who Oversteps Boundaries

They don't respect you as a parent and want to undermine your authority. They'll keep on calling/texting the children constantly when they're with you. They interrogate them about what's going on, speak negatively about you, or might even tell the children to do things that go against your rules.

Try having a respectful, but firm conversation with your ex that establishes the boundaries. Say something like: "I don't mind if you check in now and then, but constantly calling to quiz them or overstep my rules is inappropriate. We need to be a united front as parents."

Don't argue or engage further if this doesn't work. Simply reiterate the boundary and follow through—screen calls during your time, let them know you'll have the children call them back at a scheduled time. Block their number if they start harassing you.

### Example 2: The Ex Who Demands Last-Minute Changes

They think only their time matters and your schedule/life is insignificant. Your set custody schedule is a daily battle because your ex constantly tries to make you take or return the kids at wildly different times than agreed upon. This disrupts the children's routines as well as your work and personal obligations.

Calmly explain why sticking to the set schedule benefits the children as their activities aren't disrupted. See if you can compromise with slight time adjustments to meet in the middle.

Stick to your originally agreed-upon schedule. Don't deviate unless it's a real emergency. Make sure you keep documentation of the previously set times in case you need to take it to court for orders of enforcement.

### Example 3: The Ex Who Alienates the Children

This type of ex wants to turn the children against you out of bitterness or a sense of control. Your ex openly bad-mouths you to the kids, shares inappropriate details about the divorce/conflict with them, and tries to get them to choose sides.

Don't engage in that same negative behavior yourself. Reassure the children that you only want them to be safe and loved, and that it's okay to love both parents equally. Limit their exposure to the parental conflict as much as possible.

If that doesn't work do your best to maintain a secure, peaceful, and emotionally stable environment during your time with the children. Work on building their self-esteem. If severe parental alienation continues, seek legal measures.

### Example 4: The Ex Who Nickel-And-Dimes Everything

They want to maintain a sense of control and will use money as a weapon against you.

Any discussion about child-related expenses like clothes, activities, medical bills, etc. turns into an argument. Your ex questions, contests, and punishes you for every single request.

Commit to good record-keeping and documentation. Keep proof of the children's expenses and suggest a monthly budget for each parent to cover shared costs.

If it doesn't work, pay only what you are legally obligated to through child support or previous agreements. Don't respond to provocations. Children need emotional stability more than they need extra dance classes or clothes.

No matter how unreasonable or hostile an ex-partner becomes, the key is staying calm and taking the high road as the stable, nurturing parent. The children's emotional well-being has to be the top priority through the chaos.

# Parallel Parenting

Parallel parenting can be a good way to go if you're experiencing a lot of conflict while co-parenting with your narcissistic ex. It's different from regular co-parenting because you're not trying to work together as a team. Instead, each parent does their own thing when they have the kids, without bothering the other. The goal is to have as little contact and drama with your ex as possible.

Here are some key things to keep in mind with parallel parenting:

- When it's your time with the kids, you make the decisions about daily stuff like schedules, rules, and activities. Your ex doesn't get a say.

- Only communicate with your ex when you absolutely have to, like if there's a health issue or a change in plans. Keep it short and to the point and stick to texts or emails so you have a record.

- When swapping the kids, do it at a neutral place like school or daycare. This way, you don't have to see your ex and risk getting into a fight.

- Make sure you have a clear, written parenting plan that spells out each parent's responsibilities, the schedule, and how you'll handle communication and disagreements.

- If there's a school play or soccer game, each parent goes when they have the kids. You don't have to sit together and pretend to be a happy family.

- Even though you're not co-parenting, try to have some basic rules and routines that are the same at both houses. This helps the kids feel stable and secure.

- Parallel parenting means you have to let go of trying to control or change your ex. Put your energy into your own relationship with your kids, and don't bad-mouth your ex in front of them.

Parallel parenting isn't easy, and it takes a lot of self-control to bite your tongue and not get sucked into drama. But if you can make it work, it can be a good way to keep both parents involved with the kids while keeping conflict to a minimum.

# Activity: Practicing Effective Communication and Conflict Resolution

This activity will help you develop and practice effective communication and conflict resolution skills to manage high-conflict co-parenting situations.

## Materials

- pen and paper or a digital document
- timer

## Instructions

1. Identify common communication challenges:
   - List specific examples of communication breakdowns or conflicts with your co-parent.
   - Consider the language, tone, and medium (e.g. email, text, in-person) that caused these challenges.
2. Develop "I" statements:
   - Use "I" statements, which focus on your feelings and experiences rather than blame or accusations.
   - For example, instead of saying "You never listen to me," try "I feel frustrated when I don't feel heard."
3. Practice active listening:
   - Choose a role-playing scenario from your list of common communication challenges.

- Take turns with a friend or family member playing the roles of you and your co-parent.
- When in the listening role, practice
  - giving your full attention to the speaker, and maintaining eye contact
  - acknowledging the speaker's feelings and perspectives
  - asking clarifying questions
  - summarizing what you heard to make sure you've understood them correctly

4. Focus on solutions:
   - In your role-playing scenarios, practice shifting the conversation from problems to solutions.
   - Ask open-ended questions that encourage collaboration, such as "What can we do to make this situation work for the children?"
   - Brainstorm potential solutions and compromise where possible.

5. Manage emotional triggers:
   - Identify your emotional triggers during co-parenting conversations.
   - Practice deep breathing, counting to 10, or other calming techniques when triggered.
   - Use "I" statements to express your feelings calmly and assertively.

6. Set boundaries:
   - Practice setting clear, firm boundaries while you role-play certain scenarios.
   - Use phrases like "I'm not comfortable discussing that right now" or "I won't be available to attend the event."
   - Be consistent in enforcing your boundaries, even if met with resistance.

7. Take breaks when needed:

    o If a conversation becomes heated or unproductive, practice asking for a break.
    o Use a phrase like "I think we both need some time to cool off. Let's talk again in an hour."
    o Use the break to engage in self-care and emotional regulation.

8. Reflect and refine:

    o After each role-playing session, take time to reflect on where you could improve.
    o Identify any new insights or skills you gained from the practice.
    o Continuously refine your communication and conflict-resolution skills based on your experiences.

# Key Takeaways

- High-conflict parenting involves co-parenting with an uncooperative ex-partner who refuses to communicate effectively or prioritize the children's best interests.

- Common challenges include constant arguments, last-minute schedule changes, and financial disputes.

- Narcissistic rage is when a narcissistic parent explodes in uncontrolled anger over minor issues, often verbally or physically abusing the children.

- Parallel parenting involves disengaging from the other parent and making independent decisions during parenting time.

- The communication and conflict resolution activity involves identifying challenges, using "I" statements, practicing active listening, focusing on solutions, managing triggers, setting boundaries, taking breaks, and reflecting on progress.

In Chapter 7, we'll provide you with more parenting tips.

# Chapter 7:

# Parenting Tips

Lila sat at the kitchen table, head in her hands, mentally and emotionally exhausted after another difficult interaction with her ex-husband Dan. Ever since their divorce, it seemed his narcissistic tendencies had only gotten worse, especially when it came to co-parenting their two children, 9-year-old Oliver and 6-year-old Sophie.

Just this morning, Dan had sent Lila a scathing text message, criticizing her for allowing the children to sign up for after-school art classes, claiming it was a waste of time that would interfere with the strict academic regimen he insisted upon. It was also a waste of his money since he would have to pay for these classes.

His words stung, making Lila question her parenting choices momentarily. But then she took a deep breath and remembered the promise she'd made to herself the day she left Dan—that she would always put her children's well-being and happiness first, no matter what.

Lila thought back to how timid and anxious Oliver and Sophie were in the months following the divorce, having internalized the constant belittling and unrealistic expectations Dan subjected them to. It broke her heart to see their confidence and joy slowly chipped away. That's when she resolved to rebuild a home life of emotional safety, support, and child-centered nurturing for them.

Week by week, month by month, Lila kept her focus on showering her kids with unconditional love, validating their feelings, praising their efforts, and encouraging them to pursue their interests. Slowly but surely, she saw the light returning to their eyes. Oliver no longer had stomach aches before weekend visits with his dad and Sophie's night terrors lessened. They started sharing their artwork proudly, made new friends, and laughed more. Lila knew there was still healing to be done, but she could see the resilience growing in her babies.

As much as Dan tried to undermine and sabotage her relationship with the children, Lila refused to give up or sink to his level. She knew the greatest gift she could give Oliver and Sophie was her consistent, steady presence and emotional attunement to their lives.

Determined to do just this, Lila clicked her phone screen off, not bothering to respond to Dan's angry text messages. She had an art show to get to, where two bright, brave kids were waiting to proudly show her the fruits of their creative efforts. She was determined that nothing, especially Dan, was going to make her miss it.

# Parenting Tips

When you're co-parenting with a narcissistic ex, it can feel like an endless struggle to create a healthy, nurturing environment for your children. However, staying focused on your kids' needs and well-being can help them thrive despite the challenges.

The first and most important thing is to always put your children first. This means creating a home life all about their emotional and mental security, building their confidence, and fostering their happiness. It's not easy, especially when your ex is constantly trying to undermine you, but remember that your consistency and love are what your kids need most.

To provide emotional security, make sure your children feel heard and validated. Listen to their feelings without judging them and let them know it's okay to express themselves, even if they might be ashamed. Create a safe space where they can talk openly about their experiences with both parents. For example, if your child comes home upset after a visit with your ex, sit down with them and say, "I can see that you're feeling sad. Do you want to talk about what happened?" Let them share without interrupting or getting defensive.

Mental security comes from a predictable, stable environment. Always keep your promises to your children and think carefully before you promise them anything. Stick to routines as much as possible and be reliable in your words and actions. When your ex makes promises and doesn't follow through, resist the urge to bad-mouth them. Instead, focus on being the steady, dependable parent your kids can count on. For instance, if your ex frequently cancels or shows up late for their scheduled time with the kids, don't make excuses for them. Simply say, "I know it's disappointing when plans change suddenly. Let's think of something fun we can do together instead."

Building your children's confidence starts with praising their efforts and achievements, no matter how small. Encourage them to pursue their interests and passions, even if your ex disapproves. Show them that their opinions and choices matter. For example, if your child wants to take dance lessons but your ex thinks it's a waste of time, sign them up anyway and attend their recitals with enthusiasm, even if your ex refuses to do so.

Keeping your kids happy means prioritizing quality time together, filled with laughter, play, and positive experiences. Create traditions and rituals that belong just to your family unit, separate from the stress of dealing with your ex. For instance, have a weekly game night or a monthly "adventure day" where you explore new places together.

Finally, do your best to maintain a good relationship with your kids, even when your narcissistic ex tries to get in the way. Avoid arguing or speaking negatively about the other parent in front of your children. Instead, model respectful communication and boundary-setting. Remember, your kids love both their parents, and they need to know that it's okay for them to love both of you. If your ex tries to turn the kids against you, respond with love and understanding. You might say, "I know you love both me and your dad/mom, and that's okay. I will always love you no matter what."

By staying child-focused, providing security, building confidence, prioritizing happiness, and nurturing your relationship, you can help your kids navigate the challenges of having a narcissistic parent. Listed below are some ways you can achieve that.

## Create a Calm-Down Corner

Creating a special "calm-down corner" in your home is a great way to help your kids feel emotionally secure, especially when they're dealing with the stress and confusion of having a narcissistic parent. This cozy space can be a haven for whenever they need a break, feel overwhelmed, or just want some quiet time.

To make the calm-down corner inviting and comforting, choose a spot in your home that feels peaceful and private. It could be a corner of their bedroom, a little nook in the living room, or even a special tent or fort you set up together. The key is to make it a place where your child feels protected and at ease.

Fill the space with soft, comfy things like big pillows, fluffy blankets, and their favorite stuffed animals. These familiar, cozy items can help your child feel soothed and safe when upset or anxious.

Next, add some calming activities to the corner. This could include coloring books and crayons, puzzle books, or even a small sand garden with a little rake. The idea is to give your child something to focus on that helps them relax and unwind. You can even include a few squeeze balls or fidget toys to help release pent-up energy or frustration.

If your child enjoys music, consider adding headphones and an MP3 player or small speaker with a playlist of their favorite calming tunes. Soft classical music, nature sounds, or even white noise can be really helpful in creating a peaceful atmosphere.

Encourage your kids to visit their calm-down corner whenever they need it, no questions asked. Let them know that it's always okay to take a break and that you're proud of them for recognizing when they need some extra self-care.

You can even make visiting the calm-down corner a special ritual you do together. For example, when your child feels upset after a difficult interaction with their other parent, you might say, "I can see that you're feeling really sad right now. Why don't we go to your cozy corner and snuggle up with some soft blankets? We can read a story or just cuddle until you feel better."

By creating this safe, comforting space and encouraging your child to use it regularly, you're helping them build important emotional regulation skills that will serve them well throughout their lives. Plus, you're showing them that their feelings matter and that they always have a soft place to land when life gets tough.

Remember, the calm-down corner doesn't have to be perfect or fancy. The most important thing is that it feels like a special, loving space where your child can feel secure, supported, and at peace. With a little creativity and lots of love, you can create a wonderful emotional oasis for your kids in your own home.

## *Mental Security*

When you're parenting kids who have a narcissistic parent, it's extra important to create a stable, predictable environment at home. One of the best ways to do this is by setting clear, age-appropriate rules and consequences and sticking to them consistently.

Kids thrive when they know what's expected of them and what will happen if they don't follow the rules. It helps them feel safe and secure, even when other parts of their life might feel chaotic or unpredictable.

To get started, sit down with your kids and make a list of basic rules for your household. These could include things like doing homework before playtime. Keep the rules simple, clear, and age-appropriate. For younger kids, you might use pictures or charts to help them understand and remember the rules.

Next, decide on the consequences of breaking the rules. These should also be age-appropriate and related to the rule that was broken. For example, if your child doesn't clean their room when asked, they won't be able to play with their toys until their room is tidy.

It's important to be consistent with enforcing the rules and consequences. This means following through every time, even when it's hard or inconvenient. If you let things slide sometimes, your kids will get confused and won't know what to expect.

When your child does follow the rules, be sure to praise them and let them know you noticed their good behavior. You can say something like, "I'm so proud of you for being kind to your brother even when you were frustrated. Great job following our family rules!"

By establishing clear rules and consequences, you're creating a sense of structure and stability that your kids desperately need, which will help them know what to expect at your home.

In addition, by involving your kids in creating the rules and consequences, you're helping them feel a sense of ownership and responsibility. They'll be more likely to follow the rules when they've had a say in making them.

## Building Confidence and Joy

Building your children's confidence and finding ways to bring more joy and laughter into your daily life are powerful ways to help them thrive, especially when they're dealing with the challenges of having a narcissistic parent.

One simple but effective way to boost your kids' confidence is by proudly displaying their artwork, awards, and photos around your home. This sends a clear message that you value their efforts and achievements, no matter how small.

Stick their drawings on the fridge, frame and hang their paintings, or create a special shelf to showcase their trophies and ribbons. Every time your child sees their work displayed, they'll feel a little burst of pride and accomplishment.

You can also use these displays as conversation starters to celebrate your child's unique talents and interests. For example, if your child brings home a science fair ribbon, you might say, "Wow, look at this amazing ribbon! I'm so impressed by how hard you worked on your project. Tell me more about what you learned!" By showing genuine interest and enthusiasm for your child's passions, you're helping them build a strong sense of self and teaching them that their efforts matter.

Another key way to support your kids is by finding ways to infuse more joy, silliness, and laughter into your daily life together. When kids are dealing with heavy emotions or stressful situations, it's important to balance it out with plenty of positive, lighthearted moments.

One easy way to do this is to have silly dance parties in the living room. Put on some upbeat music, let loose, and have fun moving and grooving together. Don't worry about looking perfect or coordinated—the goal is just to be silly, let go, and enjoy the moment.

You can also bring more joy into your routine by baking cookies together, starting a family book club, or having regular game nights where you play your kids' favorite board games. The key is to find activities that you all enjoy and that give you opportunities to laugh, be playful, and connect positively.

These moments of joy and connection are a healing balm for kids who are dealing with the stress and confusion of having a narcissistic parent. They help remind your kids that life can be fun and happy, even when things are tough.

By making these joyful activities a regular part of your routine, you're creating positive memories and traditions that your kids will cherish for years to come. They'll look back on these moments and know that no matter the challenges, they always had a loving, supportive parent who made time for play and laughter.

Ultimately, you don't have to do anything elaborate or expensive to bring more joy and confidence into your kids' lives. The most important thing is to be present, engaged, and loving.

# Activity: Creating a Happy Memory Scrapbook

You can help your children develop joy and confidence by creating a "Happy Memory Scrapbook." This activity allows children to focus on positive experiences and memories, reinforcing their self-worth and resilience.

## *Materials*
- a scrapbook or a binder with blank pages
- photos of happy moments or experiences
- colorful paper, stickers, and other decorative items
- scissors and glue
- markers or pens

## Instructions

1. Sit down with your child and explain that you'll create a special book to celebrate all the happy moments and memories you've shared.

2. Go through photos together and select those representing joyful experiences, accomplishments, or milestones. These could include birthdays, vacations, school events, or even simple, everyday moments like playing at the park or cuddling with a pet.

3. Your child should glue the photos onto the scrapbook pages, leaving space for writing and decoration.

4. Encourage your child to decorate the pages with stickers, drawings, or anything else that makes them feel happy and proud.

5. Help your child write short captions or stories about each photo, focusing on the positive feelings and experiences associated with those moments. For example, "I felt so proud of myself when I learned to ride a bike!" or "I had the best time laughing and playing with my friends at the beach."

6. As you work on the scrapbook together, take the opportunity to praise your child's creativity, effort, and resilience. Remind them that they have the power to create joy and happiness in their life, no matter what challenges they face.

7. Once the scrapbook is complete, make a special spot to keep it where your child can easily access it. Encourage them to look through it whenever they need a reminder of their strengths, achievements, and happy memories.

8. Keep adding to the scrapbook over time as your child experiences new joyful moments and milestones. This ongoing activity will help reinforce the idea that life is full of positive experiences and that your child can create and savor happiness.

By focusing on happy memories and experiences, this activity helps children build a positive self-image and reminds them that they are loved, valued, and capable of joy.

# Key Takeaways

- When co-parenting with a narcissistic ex, stay focused on your children's needs and well-being to help them thrive despite challenges.

- Always put your children first by creating a home life focused on their emotional security, mental security, confidence, and happiness.

- Provide emotional security by listening to their feelings without judgment, validating them, and creating a safe space for them to express themselves about interactions with both parents.

- Build their confidence by praising efforts and achievements, encouraging their interests, and showing them that their opinions matter.

- Create a special "calm-down corner" with cozy elements and calming activities as a soothing retreat.

- Establish clear, age-appropriate, and consistently enforced household rules and consequences to provide stability.

- Proudly display their artwork, awards, and photos to celebrate achievements and boost confidence. Infuse daily life with silly, joyful activities.

In Chapter 8, let's look at finding healing and peace.

# Chapter 8:

# Healing and Finding Peace

Adeola took a deep breath as she stepped out of the shower, wrapping herself in a plush towel. She caught a glimpse of her reflection in the foggy mirror and paused, studying the woman staring back at her. The dark circles under her eyes and the weariness etched onto her face were reminders of the emotional turmoil she had endured during her marriage to Kwame.

For years, Adeola had walked on eggshells, her sense of self fading as a result of Kwame's manipulation, constant criticisms, and put-downs.

Even after leaving him, she had trouble envisioning a happy future without his shadow looming over her.

However, as she dried her hair and prepared for the day ahead, she felt determined once more. She knew she had to heal, not just for herself but for the sake of her two young daughters who needed her to be strong, resilient, and whole.

Adeola made a mental list of self-care activities to prioritize that day: a nourishing breakfast, a brisk walk in the park to clear her mind, and perhaps a pedicure later. She recognized that reclaiming her identity and rediscovering her worth wouldn't happen overnight, but she was committed to the process, one small step at a time.

Forgiveness wouldn't come easily, but Adeola knew she had to let go of the anger and bitterness that weighed her down. It was time to write a new chapter, one where she was the author of her own story, crafting a life that reflected her true values and aspirations.

# Why You Need to Look After Your Well-Being

Although your priority is probably the well-being of the children when leaving a narcissist, you need to look after your well-being as well.

After leaving a toxic relationship, you might feel drained and could be questioning your self-worth. You need to prioritize your well-being and start healing for the sake of your children, who have their own wounds to heal from.

When you prioritize your healing and self-care, you send a powerful message to your children that their worth is intrinsic, their emotions and experiences are valid, and they deserve to be treated with kindness, respect, and compassion.

By taking the time to nurture your mind, body, and soul, you show how important it is to take care of yourself by helping your children understand that it's not only okay but necessary to put their well-being first sometimes. This lesson is invaluable, especially for those who have grown up in an environment where their needs are consistently neglected or outright rejected.

As you work through the process of healing from narcissistic abuse, embracing self-compassion, and rediscovering your identity you're setting an example for your children. They will learn from your strength and resilience and find hope for the future.

Focusing on your own well-being will help you be the more present, attentive, and nurturing parent your children need during this turbulent time. You'll be better equipped to provide the stability, unconditional love, and emotional support they crave, helping them feel seen, heard, and valued in a way they may have never experienced.

# Self-Care Tips

Self-care gives you the energy and resilience to nurture your children through this turbulent time.

## Physical Self-Care

Physical self-care should be your priority, and it might be the easiest place to start. Making time for exercise, even if it's just a daily 20-minute walk, can boost your mood and reduce your stress levels. Activities like yoga, swimming, or cycling are also great low-impact options.

Eating well should also be a priority. Nourish your body with balanced, healthy meals packed with fruits, vegetables, lean proteins, and complex carbs. Proper nutrition will boost your energy levels. However, don't feel guilty about indulging in comfort food from time to time—after all, this freedom is what your new life is about. There's no more critical narcissist watching every bite you eat and making derogatory remarks.

You also shouldn't underestimate the power of good sleep hygiene—stick to a consistent schedule, limit your screen time before bed, and create a calming bedtime routine like taking a warm bath or enjoying a cup of milk or chamomile tea. The fact that the narcissist is no longer around to constantly pick fights and drain your energy should also help you sleep better.

## Mental Self-Care

For mental self-care, read uplifting books, podcasts, or online resources that validate your experiences and offer guidance for healing from narcissistic abuse. Starting a new hobby you've always wanted to try, like painting, gardening, learning an instrument, or taking a class, can be therapeutic and help you discover new talents you didn't know you had before. Mindfulness practices like meditation, deep breathing exercises, or simply taking a few moments each day to pause, be present, and appreciate the small joys around you, can also help you feel better about the world.

## Emotional Self-Care

Emotional self-care will help you process the complex feelings that come with extricating yourself from a narcissistic relationship.

Joining a support group, whether in-person or online, can help you connect with others who went through the same experiences and understand your journey. They can listen with empathy when you talk about your experiences, and you can do the same for them.

Write in a journal to freely express your thoughts, fears, and experiences without judgment or filter. You can write in a book like a nice leather bound journal or type away on any of your electronic devices. Write or type as slow or fast as you want, just get your thoughts out there. You never have to show it to anyone so you could even write letters to the narcissist.

Counseling could help to make sure you find a therapist who specializes in narcissistic abuse recovery. Visit Dr. Ramani Durvasula's channel on YouTube. She is an American clinical psychologist who specializes in narcissism and other personality disorders. Watching her videos and learning more can also help you decide if a psychologist is right for you.

## Social Self-Care

For social self-care, prioritize spending quality time with family and friends who uplift, support, and energize you. Their positive presence can be incredibly healing. At the same time, it's okay to say "no" to social obligations that drain you or trigger negative emotions as it's important to protect your energy. If faith is important to you, find a supportive spiritual community where you can connect, worship, and recharge.

## Me-Time

Finally, be sure to carve out regular me-time for activities you genuinely enjoy and allow you to fully relax and be present, without guilt or distraction. This could mean taking a long, luxurious bath with your favorite book and a glass of wine, getting a massage, or curling up to watch a beloved movie. If your budget allows, book a weekend getaway—even a short road trip can provide a restorative change of scenery. Don't be afraid to splurge on little luxuries that make you feel good, like fresh flowers for your home, a soft new robe, or a fun new outfit that boosts your confidence.

# Reinventing Yourself

After enduring the toxic environment of a narcissistic relationship, the prospect of reinventing yourself can feel both exhilarating and daunting. On one hand, you're free from the constant belittling, manipulation, and control that stripped away your sense of self. On the other, you may feel lost, unsure of who you truly are without the constraints and criticisms of your narcissistic partner. You need to build the self-confidence to stand on your own.

This is your chance to rediscover and reclaim the authentic version of yourself that's been suppressed for far too long. You're stepping into a new chapter, a fresh start brimming with possibilities. But where do you begin?

Start by envisioning the person you want to become. What values do you want to embody? What dreams or ambitions did you have to put aside to accommodate your partner's needs? Write them down and give yourself permission to pursue them again.

Maybe you've always longed to go back to school, switch careers, or start your own business. Perhaps you've neglected your hobbies, like painting, dancing, playing music, or reading books. It could also be that you just want to cultivate more self-confidence, assertiveness, and a stronger sense of boundaries.

Whatever your goals, take practical steps to make them a reality. Research educational programs, look for new job opportunities, or sign up for that class you've been putting off. Immerse yourself in activities that light you up and reignite those long-dormant passions.

Along the way, you may find yourself shedding old habits, patterns of thinking, or ways of being that no longer serve you. That's okay—in fact, it's part of the process. Embrace the changes, even if they feel uncomfortable at first. You're actively choosing growth and self-discovery over the stagnation and diminishment you experienced in your narcissistic relationship.

Surround yourself with supportive people who see your true worth and potential. Let go of toxic friendships or family ties that mimic the dynamics you try to escape. Seek out communities, whether in-person or online, that align with your newfound values and aspirations.

And be patient with yourself. Reinvention doesn't happen overnight. There will be setbacks, self-doubt, and days when the old patterns try to resurface. But keep putting one foot in front of the other, celebrating each small victory along the way.

You're emerging from the shadows of narcissistic abuse, ready to blossom into the fullest, most authentic expression of yourself. It's a journey of courage, self-compassion, and radical self-love. By fearlessly embracing this new chapter, you're not just reinventing your life—you're reclaiming the vibrant, empowered person you were always meant to be.

After years of being crammed into a small box of who your narcissistic ex thought you should be, you're finally ready to embrace your full, authentic self.

It will feel strange at first, letting your true self shine without your ex's constant criticism. You no longer have to try to be someone you're not. If shedding those dysfunctional habits and patterns causes discomfort, so be it—that's the price of admission to start living life for yourself.

You're cutting ties with any toxic relationships that no longer align with who you're becoming. Instead, you surround yourself with a supportive friend group who hypes you up and encourages your visions and goals.

## *Forgiving*

After dealing with your ex for so long, you're probably carrying around a lot of anger and bitterness. The selfish and manipulative way they've treated you has given you every right to be furious at them.

However, holding onto all that hatred and resentment will only hurt you in the long run. Staying stuck in that rage just gives your ex more power over your mind and healing.

Forgiveness isn't about saying what they did was acceptable or forgetting about the terrible way they acted. It's about freeing yourself from the toxic negativity weighing you down like a ball and chain. As long as you feed into that hatred, they've still got you trapped.

Each time you replay those painful memories and rage about how they wronged you, it's like taking the knife they twisted in your back and stabbing yourself with it over and over. Why keep inflicting that pain on yourself when the narcissist has likely already moved on without care? You're just giving them power over you; the narcissist probably aren't thinking of you at all when you're not with them.

Genuine forgiveness means letting go of that dark cloud of anger, one day at a time. It's choosing peace, joy, and your well-being over being a hostage to resentment. You're refusing to be a victim of the narcissist.

The forgiving process involves a lot of crying, venting, or punching pillows until the worst of the anguish passes. Be patient and compassionate with yourself.

One day those painful memories will stop replaying in your mind. The resentment that was like a weight on your chest will be gone, and you'll feel lighter.

When you find that the toxic thoughts of your ex are creeping back in, catch yourself. Envision putting them in a box, locking it up, and tossing away the key. Or lean on your friends who understand what you went through instead of bottling it up.

Just keep choosing your happiness and well-being over and over. In time, all that hatred will loosen its grip. The narcissist has already taken enough from you. Don't let them steal one more precious moment of your joy by holding onto resentment. You'll find true healing when you let hatred go.

# Activity: Creating a Self-Care Plan for Healing From a Narcissistic Relationship

This activity aims to develop a personalized self-care plan that supports your emotional healing and recovery from a relationship with a narcissist.

## *Instructions*

Take some time to consider what you need to feel supported, safe, and nurtured during your healing process. Write down your thoughts.

Create a list of activities that promote your physical, emotional, and mental well-being.

Consider the following categories:

- Physical self-care
    - Exercise (e.g., yoga, walking, dancing)
    - Healthy eating
    - Adequate sleep
    - Relaxation techniques (e.g., deep breathing, progressive muscle relaxation)
- Emotional self-care
    - Journaling
    - Creative expression (e.g., art, music, writing)
    - Spending time with supportive friends and family
    - Practicing self-compassion and positive self-talk
- Mental self-care
    - Therapy or counseling
    - Reading self-help books or articles
    - Engaging in hobbies or learning new skills
    - Mindfulness and meditation

Choose the top five to seven self-care activities that resonate with you the most and that you feel will be most beneficial for your healing.

Decide how often and when you will engage in each self-care activity. Be realistic and consider your current obligations and time constraints.

Identify any boundaries you need to set with others or yourself to protect your emotional well-being and create space for your self-care practice.

Identify trusted friends, family members, or professionals who can support you in your healing journey. Consider joining a support group for survivors of narcissistic abuse.

Begin implementing your self-care plan, and be willing to make adjustments as needed. Remember that healing is a process, and it's okay to take things one day at a time.

## Example Self-Care Plan

### Daily

- morning meditation (10 minutes)
- journaling (15 minutes)
- evening walk (30 minutes)

### Weekly

- therapy session (1 hour)
- art class (2 hours)
- coffee with a supportive friend (1 hour)

### Monthly

- massage or spa treatment
- volunteer at a local animal shelter

## Boundaries

- limited contact with ex-partner
- saying "no" to commitments that drain my energy

## Support

- weekly phone call with best friend
- attending a local support group for narcissistic abuse survivors

Your self-care plan should be tailored to your unique needs and preferences. Be patient with yourself and celebrate your progress, no matter how small. You deserve to prioritize your well-being and happiness as you heal from the trauma of a narcissistic relationship.

# Key Takeaways

- After leaving a narcissistic relationship, prioritizing your own well-being and healing is crucial for yourself and your children.

- By focusing on self-care, you model the importance of self-love, validate your experiences, and become a more present, nurturing parent.

- Reinventing yourself after a narcissistic relationship involves rediscovering your authentic self, pursuing dreams, and shedding old patterns.

# Bonus Resources

There are tons of resources that can help you process what you've been through, build your self-esteem, and move forward in a healthy way. From online support groups where you can connect with people who get what you're going through, to apps that make it easy to access professional help, to inspiring books and blogs full of practical advice—there's a wealth of support available. We include some examples below.

## Supportive Resources to Help You Recover

There are a variety of resources that can help you with your recovery and keep you on the right track. Let's take a look at some of them.

### Affirmation Cards

You can find free printable affirmation cards on websites like ThinkUp (thinkup.me), which offers a variety of themed card decks with positive quotes and mantras. For example, their "Self-Love" deck includes cards with messages like "I am worthy of love and respect" and "I choose to be kind to myself."

### Phone Wallpapers

Websites like Canva (canva.com) offer a wide selection of free, customizable phone wallpapers with inspiring quotes and beautiful images. You can browse their "Motivational Wallpapers" collection and download designs that resonate with you. Zedge (zedge.net) is another popular platform for finding uplifting wallpapers.

## Printable Art

Etsy (etsy.com) has a vast collection of downloadable art prints with encouraging sayings. For instance, the shop "HealingWallprints" offers a print that reads, "I am not what happened to me. I am what I choose to become." You can purchase, download, and print these designs to display in your home.

## Custody Battle Journal

One option is the *High Conflict Custody Battle Journal* by Megan Hunter, available on Amazon. This journal is specifically designed for parents navigating difficult custody situations and includes guided prompts, tips for effective communication, and self-care exercises. There are a number of Custody Battle journals available on the site.

## Custody Calendar

The "Divorce Calendar" by Co-Parenting Planner (coparentingplanner.com) is a comprehensive tool for managing custody schedules, visitation, and important dates. It's available as a printable PDF or can be synced with your digital calendar.

## Apps and Online Resources

- Online Support Groups: In addition to Reddit's r/NarcissisticAbuse, Facebook also has private groups like "Narcissistic Abuse Support Group" and "Thriving After Narcissistic Abuse" where survivors can connect and share experiences.

- Therapy Apps: BetterHelp (betterhelp.com) and TalkSpace (talkspace.com) offer virtual therapy sessions with licensed professionals who specialize in helping people recover from narcissistic abuse. You can access these services through their websites or mobile apps.

- Meditation Apps: Insight Timer (insighttimer.com) is a free app with a library of guided meditations, including sessions focused on healing from toxic relationships and building self-compassion.
- DocuSAFE App: This app (docusafe.com) allows you to securely store and organize important documents related to your custody case, such as court orders, communication records, and expense receipts. It's available for both iOS and Android devices.

## Books

- *The Narcissist's Playbook* by Dana Morningstar: This book offers practical strategies for coping with narcissistic abuse, setting boundaries, and rebuilding your life after a toxic relationship.
- *Divorcing a Narcissist* by Tina Swithin: Written by a survivor of a high-conflict divorce, this book guides you on navigating the legal system, protecting your children, and maintaining your sanity while sorting out your life.

## Specialists in Narcissism: YouTube Channels

There are also some excellent YouTube channels from specialists that offer valuable insights and strategies for recovering from narcissistic abuse.

Dr. Ramani Durvasula is a licensed clinical psychologist and professor of psychology, who holds in-depth discussions on narcissistic personality disorder and its impact on relationships. Her channel also provides practical advice for survivors and is a go-to resource for people who want to understand and heal from narcissistic abuse.

Dr. Les Carter has over 30 years of experience as a counselor and shares his expertise on dealing with narcissistic behavior, setting boundaries, and developing healthy communication skills. His videos are filled with relatable examples and actionable tips.

Surviving Narcissism (Dr. Les Carter and Dr. Michelle Piper) is a collaborative channel, where Dr. Carter teams up with Dr. Michelle Piper, a psychologist who specializes in helping people recover from toxic relationships. Together, they dive into topics like co-parenting with a narcissist, narcissistic family dynamics, and the healing process.

Dr. Todd Grande is a licensed professional counselor and therapist who offers informative videos on various mental health topics, including narcissistic personality disorder. He breaks down complex psychological concepts in an easy-to-understand manner and provides insights into the narcissistic mind.

Rebecca Zung, Esq.: While not a mental health professional, Rebecca Zung is a divorce attorney who specializes in helping people navigate high-conflict divorces with narcissistic partners. Her channel offers valuable legal advice and strategies for dealing with narcissists in the context of divorce and co-parenting.

By subscribing and tuning in regularly to these channels, you can gain a deeper understanding of narcissistic behavior, learn coping strategies, and feel empowered in your healing journey.

# Conclusion

As we come to the end of this book, I want to remind you of how far you've come. You've taken the courageous step of leaving a toxic relationship, and you've committed to creating a better life for yourself and your children. It hasn't been easy, but you've armed yourself with the knowledge, tools, and strategies needed to navigate the challenges of co-parenting with a narcissistic ex.

Remember, healing is a journey, and it's okay to take it one day at a time. Celebrate your progress, no matter how small, and be kind to yourself along the way. You're not just surviving, you're thriving, and that's a testament to your incredible strength and resilience.

As you move forward, keep setting goals for yourself and envisioning the life you've always dreamed of. You have the power to make it a reality. Surround yourself with supportive people who understand your journey and can offer encouragement and guidance when you need it.

Most importantly, never forget that you deserve happiness, peace, and love. By breaking free from the cycle of narcissistic abuse, you're not only reclaiming your own life but also giving your children the gift of a healthier, more stable home environment.

You've got this, and I'm cheering you on every step of the way. Remember, you are not alone and are worthy of the beautiful life that awaits you.

If you've found this book helpful, I would be grateful if you could take a moment to leave a review. Your feedback helps other readers who may be going through similar experiences find the support and guidance they need. Thank you for sharing your strength with others.

# About The Author

Olivia Clarke is a shining light in the world of mental health. She understands what it's like to struggle because she's been through a lot herself, including abuse and trauma. But instead of letting it keep her down, Olivia used her experiences to become a stronger, more understanding person.

She now uses her knowledge of psychology and her own journey to help others. When she writes her books, she reaches out a hand to guide and support her readers as she shares tips and advice that are easy to understand and use in real life.

Olivia has a special way of connecting with people, whether they're kids or adults. When you read her words, you can feel how much she cares. She writes with so much honesty and heart that it's easy to relate to what she's saying.

Even though Olivia is kind and gentle, she's also a powerful force. She shows us that no matter what we've been through, we have the strength inside us to heal and grow. Olivia inspires people to believe in themselves and to stand up for their own well-being.

Get the latest on new releases, free content and special promotions sent straight to your inbox! Sign up for our monthly news letter to stay updated with Rocket Publishing Group and Olivia Clarke.

# References

Biggers, L. (2022, December 15). *9 signs of narcissistic personality disorder*. Duke Health. https://www.dukehealth.org/blog/9-signs-of-narcissistic-personality-disorder

Brennan, D. (2020, December 2). *Narcissism: symptoms and signs*. WebMD. https://www.webmd.com/mental-health/narcissism-symptoms-signs

Connell, L.K. (n.d.). *What are flying monkeys and how to deal with them?* https://www.laurakconnell.com/blog/flying-monkeys

Cooks-Campbell, A. (2022, April 28). *How to deal with difficult people — without harming your mental health*. Betterup. https://www.betterup.com/blog/how-to-deal-with-difficult-people

Mayo Clinic. (2023, April 6). *Narcissistic personality disorder - symptoms and causes*. Mayo Clinic. https://www.mayoclinic.org/diseases-conditions/narcissistic-personality-disorder/symptoms-causes/syc-20366662

Media, K. C. (2023, November 21). *Signs you had a narcissistic parent, and how it may have impacted your own development*. Katie Couric Media. https://katiecouric.com/lifestyle/parenting/signs-you-had-a-narcissistic-parent/

Newport Institute. (2022, November 1). *How Having a Narcissistic Parent Impacts Young Adult Mental Health*. Newport Institute. https://www.newportinstitute.com/resources/mental-health/narcissistic-parent/

Raypole, C. (2020, July 27). *12 signs you might have narcissistic victim syndrome*. Healthline. https://www.healthline.com/health/narcissistic-victim-syndrome

Rensburg, G. J. V. (2021, October 26). *What is meant by the term "flying monkeys" in narcissism?* White River Manor. https://www.whiterivermanor.com/news/flying-monkeys-in-narcissism/

Ripes, J. (2021, April 21). *13 tips for how to heal from a toxic relationship.* Modern Intimacy. https://www.modernintimacy.com/13-tips-for-how-to-heal-from-a-toxic-relationship/

Robinson, K. M. (n.d.). *What to do if you're co-parenting with a narcissist.* WebMD. https://www.webmd.com/mental-health/features/narcissistic-coparent

Robinson, L., Segal, J., & Jaffe, J. (2021). *How attachment styles affect adult relationships.* HelpGuide.org. https://www.helpguide.org/articles/relationships-communication/attachment-and-adult-relationships.htm

Smith, M., & Robinson, L. (2019, March 21). *Narcissistic Personality Disorder.* HelpGuide.org. https://www.helpguide.org/articles/mental-disorders/narcissistic-personality-disorder.htm

Thomas, N. (n.d.). *10 Signs of a narcissistic parent, & How to deal with them.* Choosing Therapy. https://www.choosingtherapy.com/narcissistic-parent/

Made in United States
Troutdale, OR
08/26/2024

22349786R00066